BUYING YOUR NEXT CAR
your questions answered

BUYING YOUR NEXT CAR
your questions answered

Philip Turner

Otter Publications
Chichester, England

First published in 1996 by **Otter Publications**, 5 Mosse Gardens, Fishbourne, Chichester, West Sussex, PO19 3PQ.

DISCLAIMER
While every effort has been made to ensure that the contents of this book are accurate, neither the author nor publisher accepts any liability for any losses or consequential losses incurred by any person(s) or vehicle(s) as a direct or indirect result of reading or acting upon the advice contained within the text. In addition, it is recommended that a degree of caution be exercised when standing near to any moving or stationary mechanical or structural vehicle parts - particularly if hot - and that the reader shows some restraint when conducting any of the tests that follow on another's car. Readers should also be reminded that it would not be wise to rely upon the use of a simple wheel jack to support a vehicle while inspecting underneath: axle stands, driving ramps, or a professional hoist or garage inspection pit should be used instead.

British Library Cataloging in Publication Data
A CIP record for this book is available from the British Library.
ISBN 1 899053 07 7

Acknowledgements
I would like to thank the following sources in particular for their assistance and inspiration during the compilation of this book:
Phil Mobsby - Ford Technical, Walsall. Alan Welsh, Automobile Association (Inspections) HPI Equifax plc. DVLA, Swansea. Bromley and Lewisham Trading Standards. Lou Pinter, and Bob McCready. The publisher would like to thank Duncan Callow, legal expert for What Car? magazine for his advice and help with Chapter 5.

Text design by Angela Hutchings.
Cover design by Jim Wilkie.
Printed and bound in Great Britain by Hartnolls Ltd., Bodmin.
Distributed in the UK by Grantham Book Services Ltd., Isaac Newton Way, Alma Park Industrial Estate, Grantham, Lincolnshire, NG31 9SD.
The Otter Publications logo is reproduced from original artwork by David Kitt.

Table of Contents

For David Tweddle

Introduction

Buying a secondhand car can be an experience fraught with difficulty and one which at the same time raises dozens of tough questions such as: Which model should I buy? What about engine size, economy and performance? What of depreciation and running costs? Will a diesel model mean cheaper driving?

What do I need to know about turbo models and exhaust catalysts? How important is a car's colour in determining its selling price? Are some colours and specifications very hard to resell? How will I know if the vehicle has been stolen, clocked, accident-damaged, or whether it is still under a finance agreement? Furthermore, what can I do if I've already bought a car like this? Are motor auctions to be avoided or can I save myself several hundreds of pounds by purchasing this way? Which are the dealers to avoid and which to trust? How will the law protect me if I choose to buy a car privately?

These questions and many more important ones like them are answered directly in order to strengthen your position when buying your next car(s) and, while at the same time, helping you to avoid some of the more expensive mistakes that can snag even the experienced used car buyer.

Readers requiring more comprehensive advice are referred to the author's book: *Caution! Used Cars - a step by step guide to buying a better used car and selling the one you own.* (SPA Ltd.) ISBN 1 85421 137 4, £6.95.

"She's a good runner, low mileage, excellent economy and a unique on-board entertainment system.........!"

Chapter 1

How To Choose Your Car

Q1. Why buy a used car?
Apart from the obvious initial price differential between new and used cars, a used car will be correspondingly cheaper to insure as its replacement value diminishes.

As we will see a little later, depreciation on a car is usually at its worst during the first year, levelling off after about three. Buying a car at three years old and then selling after a further three or four will lose you far less money than if you were to sell the car having bought it from new. Many niggling (and even more serious dealer "recall category") faults should have been spotted and rectified under the warranty period of the initial keeper's ownership. Finally, the increasing trend of the main franchised dealer "approved used car" schemes has already demonstrated measurable savings over brand new models sold from the showroom.

Q2. What are some of the most common pitfalls when buying a used car?
Firstly, the "impulse" purchase. That is, a lack of any clear idea of which type of car to buy and which often leads to the purchase of something either too expensive or impractical (or both) for one's needs. For example, a 90/G 1.8L Ford Sierra hatchback is the car you know you needed, whereas a 79/V BMW 7-series is the car you actually bought. By allowing yourself to "fall in love" with a particular model, you run the risk of becoming blind to its faults, and so lower your standards of expectation to fit that example. Only days later does the

true extent of the mechanical and structural condition - along with the potentially horrendous insurance and running costs - become apparent.

Secondly, there may be a lack of product knowledge. Buying the right car has more to do with the proper research of likely running costs than simply going by the windscreen sticker price. Determine the cost of insurance, fuel consumption (particularly for larger-engined cars likely to return only modest mpg figures); service, maintenance and repair costs; service parts prices and availability, and whether used parts, mechanicals or body panels can be obtained from local breakers yards. The temptingly low forecourt price of a 1985/C V12 Jaguar Sovereign could turn out to be one of the most expensive vehicles you ever bought.

Finally, there may be a general lack of concern for the car's history; that is, its maintenance whilst in former ownership: service history, past MOT and repair documentation, along with accurate mileage verification. How **did** the previous owner(s) drive and care for the car you're about to purchase ?

Q3. What is the full range of outlets for buying a car and what are the pros and cons of each?

Main franchised dealership
The most expensive option but usually for good reason. The cars offered for sale can be some of the best available and may be sold under dealer "approved used car schemes" e.g. Ford Direct, Vauxhall Network Q etc., are typically under four years old, come with full service histories, and therefore warranted mileages, balance of the manufacturer's guarantee or other mechanical breakdown insurance or warranty package, independent AA/RAC presale inspection, and up to a 30 day exchange plan. The pre-delivery structural and mechanical inspection is also very thorough and comprehensive and, for all this peace of mind, you will pay a higher premium for the car.

Specialist dealer
Staffed by former main dealers with a thorough knowledge of a limited product range e.g. Porsche 911, 944 and 928; Ferrari, Jaguar etc., and can offer competitive service. On the minus side, specialist dealers may be scattered far and wide geographically.

Smaller, independent (non-franchised) dealership
The dealer with the most varied reputation - bad ones are not hard to find! A wider range of vehicle age, type, and consistency of preparation

is common and whilst consumer protection ought to be every bit as good as that offered by a main dealer outfit, frequently traders might try to get away with verbal guarantees and much corner-cutting at the lower end of the trade.

Private sales
A more attractive proposition for the potential buyer since the vendor has few overheads and doesn't need to provide many guarantees. Therefore, the asking price can be lower than top dealer retail. The private sale also allows you to vet the current owner which can reveal almost as much about the car's driving life and recent history as a mechanical inspection. On the negative side, consumer protection for the private buyer is currently limited to little more than the seller's accurate description of the vehicle and, in addition, cars advertised privately tend to sell quickly if in good condition.

Auctions
Large, professionally-run sites such as ADT, Central Motor Auctions, or National Car Auctions offer generally better cars comprising hundreds of popular (ex-fleet) vehicles such as Vectras, Cavaliers, Mondeos and Sierras, VW Passats, Rover Montegos, Peugeot 405s and Nissan Primeras all under one roof, which helps to keep travel, telephone and car-buying literature expenses to a minimum. Purchasing the right sort of car (see Chapter 7), can save you as much as 30% off the forecourt retail price of like models offered by the dealers. In other words, you can buy here at trade prices, too. Consumer protection via the Auction Indemnity Scheme, equivalent to the standard HPI check, will verify the vehicle's legal status - more than can be said for the private purchase. Also, on cars under five years old, an after sale test drive is usually permitted. On the minus side, opportunities for a proper inspection may be limited to a cursory assessment of the vehicle's exterior since, when bidding commences, cars rarely remain "under the hammer" for more than a couple of minutes. Secondly, any recourse on an older, unwarranted vehicle is likely to be slim.

Q4. Are there any other, less conventional places I can buy a car?
Another, source of "bargain-priced" used cars can be found in the form of the car leasing companies who will have supplied thousands of cars to the company fleets, self-employed individuals, contractors etc., and which will almost always have had a maintenance agreement written into the contract. The value of this is that the cars will have built up a service history from day one (i.e. since new), a mileage that can

therefore be guaranteed and the cars themselves will be typically no older than three to four years each. The most popular disposal route for ex-lease models is via the auctions although, more recently, lease companies have begun selling to the public direct.

Whilst not a selling point that there may have been several owner/keepers of the car before you (for example, you may be the vehicle's fourth, fifth or even sixth actual keeper), your name will probably appear as only the second owner in the logbook (V5) after the lease company, although the details of all previous keepers should be made available to you upon request.

Q5. Are there any particularly good times of year to buy used cars?

Yes. The best times to buy usually coincide with the times during which many people trade in their old cars against new ones, in particular in August with the advent of the new registration letter and, to a lesser extent, in January when the new vehicle will be registered in the current year. Used dealer stock will be highest and perhaps cheapest at these times. The Motor Show in October is another time during which dealer trade-ins are likely to be high since people may be persuaded to buy new(er) models then.

The trade also slackens markedly in Winter and it is at this time that your negotiating power will be at its greatest, particularly when buying sports models and convertibles. Conversely, buying at peak times such as during the Summer will mean you'll be paying that much more for the same car because of increased demand.

Q6. What influences do the purchases by the company fleets exert on the sale of used cars?

Approximately 75% of the new car market is currently occupied by the car rental and company fleets who may purchase their stock direct at discounts of anything up to 40%+. It follows that these cars cannot be worth any more than this amount when traded in some three to four years later and so their depreciation is said to have been high. The *residual* or resale value of the ex-company/rental car is further hit due to the fleets choosing to dispose of their vehicles at auction (this is done for simple convenience on the one hand, and also because they can afford to sell their cars without reserve - see Chapter 7). Meanwhile, it is the private motorist who, at best, is only likely to obtain an 10% discount (and therefore ends up helping subsidise the huge discounts awarded the fleets), who will lose out come trade-in time when he finds the same model of car has depreciated to less than half its list price (original value) in only three years.

Q7. What exactly is a "nearly new" car?

It is an open secret that many of the volume manufacturers have been registering a proportion of their brand new stock in the names of fictitious customers (real names, perhaps, but not genuine customers) in order to maintain their market share and for which the participating dealer receives a bonus. These same "pre-registered", but as yet unsold cars which may record little more than a delivery mileage, may be presented as, "cancelled fleet orders", "low mileage ex-demonstrators", "nearly new, late plate" models, or "service exchanges" (those cars returned under the 30 day exchange plan offered under many dealer approved used car schemes), or even, "finance company repossessions" or vehicles returned under the dealer's Personal Contract Purchase scheme.

Almost all cars in the categories listed above can be either entered at auction or sold more profitably to the public as an approved used car. For the reasons outlined in **Q3**, buying a nearly-new car can provide many of the advantages of buying a brand new car, yet at a secondhand price. However, the net effect of the nearly-new car is to depress the retail values of genuine used stock.

Q8. In general, how can I tell a good dealer from a bad one?

The impression of the dealer's showroom or forecourt will often give a good idea since large sums of money invested is a sign that he is intent on staying put and building a reputation for repeat business. Smart reception areas, wall-to-wall carpeting, "free" cups of coffee, comprehensive workshop facilities and, of course, a decent selection of well-presented, late model cars would also imply better recourse than the run-down portacabin sited on a strip of land upon which is ranged an assortment of indifferently prepared vehicles of varying vintage and which are offered at somewhat reduced prices. Ask yourself the following questions:

Does the salesman try to sell you a car on positive attributes?

- One owner from new, full service history, guaranteed mileage, new MOT.
- AA or RAC presale inspection.
- Balance of the manufacturer's warranty and 30 days in which to return the car if not satisfied **or,**

Does he try to sell the car on less tangible merits?

- Low mileage.
- Expensive stereo/CD system.
- Bodykits and spoilers.
- Low profile tyres and oversize alloy wheels.
- A 12-month mechanical breakdown insurance at a price to suit your pocket?

What is the salesman's knowledge of the car's he's selling?

- Is he quite familiar with the engine and specification particulars or do you know the detail better than he?
- How keen is the dealer to sell you any car today even if clearly not a particularly suitable model? A better dealer might actually prefer to lose your business today than force upon you the wrong car and risk his reputation and future business.

Q9. How does a car's registration letter affect its future value?

The difference in price between, say, a 1996/N model registered on 31st July and an identical 1996/P model registered on 1st August can, depending on the model, be as high as £3,000. However, this differential will become less pronounced as the cars age and, in many cases, you can use this to your advantage by buying the "older" July registration at a discount and then selling on again some five or so years later when the gap in value between the "N" and "P" registrations has all but closed. The motor trade, however, will insist that it is the *year* of registration that is the more important when buying or selling and can be illustrated by the following example:

A 1993/L vehicle registered on 31st December will, on paper, appear to be a whole year older than an identical model registered but a few hours later on January 2nd, 1994 despite them both carrying the same "L" registration prefix. Buying the "older" registration at a sizeable discount should easily offset any losses if and when the car is sold several years later. If you were intending to keep the vehicle for only a year or two before selling on, it would be better to have purchased the January-registered model.

Q10. Should I avoid buying a car no longer in production?
Not at all. In fact, the longer a car's production run the better its track record. What you need to establish beforehand are the years in which the build quality (paint finish, body work, for instance) was suspect and in which years mechanical problems such as the steering, suspension or braking mechanisms might have resulted in a recall by the manufacturer (and then to determine that the repair work was actually carried out).

By the end of a car's production run, many of the glitches and teething troubles associated with early development will have been worked out so that later examples should represent the peak of development for the model.

Another good reason for choosing an older model is that the manufacturer will often still supply mechanical parts for what can be up to twenty years from the time the model ceased production. If the car was at all popular, having sold in sufficiently large numbers, then many (local) breakers yards will become an additional plentiful source of cheap used parts.

Q11. What is meant by the term "economical life" when applied to a car?
Put simply, the economical life of a car can be defined in terms of the amount of use you can take from it without having to stretch to expensive mechanical replacements outside of regular, routine service items such as exhausts, brake pads, clutches, tyres, or oils and filters or any general ignition components essential for long engine life. Engines, transmissions (including gearboxes and axles), major drive train components, and body panels need particular care when inspecting for faults since they can greatly affect the vehicle's value at resale.

Q12. What is meant by depreciation, and how can I limit its effects?
Depreciation represents the inevitable loss in value of a vehicle from new. Immediately a car is registered, it begins to lose value, with most cars shedding between about one third and a half of their list price within three to five years - the most severe depreciation occurring inside the first year. In addition to oversupply (**Q7**), depreciative losses become two-fold:

1. The set "on the road" charges that cover the combined manufacturer and dealer profits (around 35%); delivery charges (up

to £600); road tax (currently £135); number plates and VAT, most of which would be difficult to pass on to successive buyers.
2. Losses due to the fall in demand of the vehicle as it moves out of fashion - this factor, in particular, determines the overall residual (or resale) value for any model.

Not all cars depreciate in the same way or to the same extent. For example, a Mercedes-Benz 190, 200E saloon, or 300TE estate car may lose little more than 15% of its list value in the first year. The vehicle not only has exceptionally good build quality, but also several other positive associations that many believe will enhance their own image e.g. the suggestion of wealth, success in business life, sporting personality etc. The Renault 21, on the other hand, an altogether more mainstream design suffers such horrific depreciation due to its lack of desirability that in just under four years, the saloon model had managed to shed nearly 75% of its original value. *Clearly, such a car would only be worth buying as a used car.* Among other examples of rapidly depreciating cars include many Eastern Bloc makes: FSO, Lada, Skoda, and also older Fiat and Seat models.

Depreciation can also be limited by controlling the availability of an already popular make or model e.g. the much sought-after Toyota MR2 and Mazda MX-5 sports cars are subjected to strictly limited import quotas so that in each case the values of secondhand examples are kept artificially buoyant; a good example of a slow depreciator would be the hand-built Morgan Plus 4 which actually appreciates in value! However, since depreciation affects almost all cars to a greater or lesser extent, the used car buyer might do well to choose either a new or nearly new model that holds its value extremely well, in which depreciative losses are kept to a minimum, or else a vehicle that has already reached the lowest point on its depreciation curve and so, realistically, cannot lose very much more.

Q13. How important is the choice of colour when determining a car's asking price?

It is no exaggeration to say that the right colour will help to sell a car, indeed, the stronger, more popular colours rated by the trade include metallic reds, whites, blacks, silvers and even some greens helping to add several hundreds of pounds to the car's value. Duller, solid colours, on the other hand, including browns, beiges, pale blues and greens, and yellows (except sports cars) often lead to selling difficulties.

Of greater significance, is the overall package of colour, engine size and specification. It would be generally much easier, and more profitable to resell a red 2.0 litre four-door Ford Sierra Ghia than its equivalent two-door base ('L' specification) model finished in beige and equipped with the under-powered 1.3 litre engine.

Q14. Should I go ahead and buy a car and then have it resprayed if I can't find the colour I want?

This is not a good idea since, working on the basis of approximately £85 per panel, a good respray will easily cost you several hundred pounds thus eating into the savings you would have made by purchasing the car in the less popular colour at the lower price. Bear in mind that a quality respray should also include some "invisible" areas such as under the bonnet, inside the boot and along the door shuts and bodypillars, all of which will add to the cost.

A cheaper respray - known as a "blow over" - will be anything but permanent, tending to crack and flake within, perhaps, a matter of months. Moreover, is the poorer workmanship associated with the cheaper respray likely to pose problem questions when you wish to resell?

Q15. Should I buy a diesel model for improved economy?

Not necessarily. On the one hand many diesel engines - when coupled to a turbocharger - are certainly able to match the performance of their petrol equivalents and, since diesel fuel is that much cheaper and arguably more efficient than regular four-star, there are grounds for claiming improved economy.

Q16. Upon which factors does insurance grouping depend?

Insurance group ratings are subject to many factors, quite a few of which will be personal to you. These include: driver age (or ages, if more than one person is to be included on the policy), and past driving record (including any accidents, convictions, licence points gained etc.); the age and hence replacement cost of the car if stolen, accident-damaged or vandalised; whether the car is right or left-hand drive and whether intended for full business use or merely social, domestic and pleasure cover; if comprehensively insured to embrace any and every potential risk or whether limited to the more minimal (and, for older vehicles, the more sensible) third party, fire and theft option.

The vehicle's body style and engine size will play a critical part and can be aptly illustrated by the difference in risk between a 2.8i Ford Capri with bodykit and spoilers and the equivalent 1.3 litre base model.

- Will the car be seen as a likely target for thieves (compare again the two Capris above)?
- Is the car equipped with an alarm, immobiliser or other insurance company-approved deterrent?
- Is the vehicle safely housed in a garage overnight or simply left parked out on the street (the full postcode now also needs to be taken into account)?
- What of the likely cost of repairs and the expense and availability of body panels?
- Have the engine or bodywork been even sparingly modified?
- Have any aftermarket (and, therefore, non-standard) extras been fitted, e.g. spoilers, front aprons, sideskirts and farings, blackened windscreens, ex-factory fitted sunroofs or alloy wheels?

All of these could be seen by an insurance company as being likely to increase the risk of theft and would need to be declared. Finally, is cover required for additional items such as windscreens (usually only obtainable with comprehensive policies), stereos and/or mobile phones although cover for the latter two may be standard?

Since any insurance quote will be subject to many of the above risks, and which may differ in priority from one insurance company to the next, the motorist would be best advised to gather as many quotes as possible to obtain the most competitive premium.

Q17. What are the main bodyshell types available?
There are five basic categories of car body type:

1. Two and four-door saloons.
2. Three and five-door hatchbacks.
3. Estate cars (or station wagons).
4. Sports cars, including coupes, cabriolets and convertibles.
5. All-terrain and multi-purpose vehicles comprising People Carriers and four-wheel drive/off-road vehicles.

Several body styles incorporate overlapping features, for example, an Audi Quattro uses a sports coupe body, high performance (20-valve) turbo-charged engine; an opening rear hatch (tailgate), and some four-wheel drive capability useful for when driving in adverse weather conditions.

Q18. Is it better to borrow money to buy the car or pay by cash?
For lower-priced cars, under about £3,000, certainly it would be better to pay in cash since, if for no better reasons, you will own immediate

title to the vehicle and not actually owe anybody any interest. What has to be borne in mind with the purchase of any car - new or used - is that it is a constantly depreciating asset, so that were you to take out a loan for, say, £5,300 over a three year term, at the end of that term the car would not be worth the £5,000+ you'd initially borrowed (and are still paying off) but is likely to have depreciated to more than that value.

If you do borrow money, whether from a finance house, dealer, bank, building society or personal loan, be sure to obtain and compare the APR (Annual Percentage Rate) for each source which simply ensures that you're able to contrast the various interest rates on an equal footing. Dealer finance, incidentally, will stipulate that you take out fully comprehensive motor insurance working out at perhaps several hundred pounds dearer than the third party, fire and theft coverage you had originally budgeted for. In many cases a cash, or part-cash payment may still be a good way to obtain a discount.

Q19. What happens if the car is already subject to an existing finance agreement and how can I avoid this?
Any vehicle sold by a dealer from his premises is almost certain to have been cleared through HPI Equifax (a vehicle status check now available to the public for £28.50 a time) to ensure, amongst other things, that the car is free from any existing credit arrangement, or for the dealer to make good prior to reselling the car to a third party. If you were unfortunate enough to have bought such a car at auction, you would still have been covered by, and refunded through, the Auction Indemnity Scheme - a compulsory one-off payment for the HP check made at the point of purchase (see **Q3**).

By far the greatest problem area, as far as outstanding finance is concerned, rests with the private sale where compulsory indemnities do not exist although, of course, you may always pay for the HPI check yourself. Have the seller put in writing that, to the best of his or her knowledge, the vehicle is not subject to any existing credit agreement and get them to sign and date the disclaimer. Until such time as the recording of finance company details on the logbook becomes a legal requirement, it remains only for those cars sold subject to a lease agreement that would be repossessed in the event of an unauthorised sale, while those vehicles sold subject to a straightforward hire purchase contract would normally entitle the buyer to retain the car had he bought in innocence.

Q20. Is there a cooling off period when buying on credit?
You may have a period of up to about fourteen days in which to cancel once you have signed the purchase order for the car. However, the

'cooling off' relates only to the finance part of the deal and not the transaction as a whole. You might be permitted to change your mind about the car itself though had you taken delivery of it away from the dealership premises and then discovered that it came with either a different engine size or type, colour or indeed specification to that originally agreed.

Q21. Are 0% financing schemes a good idea?
Zero per cent financing is a ploy frequently engaged by dealers - of both new and used cars - to give the impression of discounting the asking price but without really doing so. Since the dealer elects to subsidise the interest payments, you will likely forfeit any discount and, in addition, be required to pay up to twice the usual deposit (around 50% rather than the more usual 25-30% on a typical finance deal), and then have to repay the balance of the loan within a year instead of the usual two, three or, perhaps, four year term.

There are two main reasons, incidentally, why cars are sold under zero per cent finance schemes and neither of them are particularly encouraging.

1. The car is being "run out" in time for replacement by a facelift model, for example, in the way that in 1993 the Vauxhall Corsa replaced the older, outgoing Nova which dealers would have been keen to clear from their existing stocks.
2. The car is not selling as well as expected. The Fiat Croma, launched in 1986 to compete as a fleet car alongside the Ford Sierra, Vauxhall Cavalier etc. was never really a strong contender and Fiat dealers would have been keen to move existing stock on more cheaply than to have them clutter the showrooms.

Model popularity has important resale consequences. If a car is slow to sell when new, it will be all the more difficult to sell as a used car unless heavily discounted. Cashback incentives of up to £500 or so, and particularly on limited edition models, are a further indication of a car the dealer is keen to sell.

Q22. How do Personal Contract Purchases (PCPs) work?
Personal Contract Purchases are offered by an increasing number of franchised dealers of which Ford Options, Vauxhall Choices, and Peugeot Passport are perhaps the best known and, to date, have been limited to new car deals. An important point to remember is that the PCP is simply another way by which a dealer is able to rent a car out

(such that the lessee pays the depreciation on the vehicle over the agreed fixed term), and then sell it again as an approved used vehicle. The options are as follows:

1. You use your existing car as a deposit and then hire/rent the brand new model for a term of up to twenty-six months while all you pay is the monthly depreciation. Since this can work out considerably cheaper than a typical hire purchase arrangement on an identical car, a more up-market model can be offered for the same money. You do not actually get to own the car and, at the end of the two or so years, you return it to the dealer and, subject to the mileage and condition falling within pre-determined limits, you walk away with nothing further to pay.
2. At the end of the term (and subject to the same vehicle mileage and condition criteria), you may trade the model in for another and begin the cycle over again.
3. You could purchase the vehicle at the end of the term. When the car is initially leased to you, the dealer determines what is referred to as its guaranteed future minimum value and which takes into account the anticipated depreciation for the lease period. If you wanted to purchase the car, you would simply pay this amount (or "balloon" payment, as it is nicknamed) at the end of the term.

Although still in its infancy, the system has found much favour with self-employed individuals, contractors and employees who have opted for a cash sum in view of the recent changes in company car tax liability. An immediate advantage of the PCP is that since you are not actually buying the car in the first instance, you do not have the responsibility of selling it when you decide to change.

Q23. What makes the ideal used car purchase?
A "clean title" is a must. You need to be absolutely sure that:

• The vehicle is actually the vendor's to sell
• It is entirely free of financial ties
• It has been neither stolen or else poorly reconstructed following a serious accident.

A full service history is highly recommended. For peace of mind, it is worth knowing that the vehicle has received regular, frequent oil and filter changes; timing belt changes (on OHC engined models) and, with the exception of those engine configurations using hydraulic tappets, that the valve clearances have been periodically checked, adjusted and reset as necessary. Old MOTs, and invoices for repairs and replacement service items (including exhausts, tyres and the like) can all help verify the vehicle's odometer reading. Thirdly, buying a car that can be resold easily. Remember what was said in **Q13** about mainstream engine size, colour and specification.

Chapter 2

Finding A Genuine Used Car

Q24. Which documents should I ask to see first?
Usually the registration document, called the V5 (still referred to as the vehicle's log book); and, if the car is more than three years old, a valid MOT certificate. You may choose to ask the seller for further identification (typically a driving licence or original bill of sale for the car) which would help prove the car is in fact theirs to sell. Later on you will want to see any service and previous MOT history that the car may have accumulated.

Q25. What is the difference between the owner of a vehicle and its keeper?
Usually only a very subtle one and, in the huge majority of cases where private individuals are concerned, nothing at all since most of the keepers listed on the top left-hand corner of the V5 actually own the car, too.

In a number of other instances, a car may be owned by a company fleet, driving school or car rental agency or, indeed, by any other individual such as the head of a family even though the vehicle is habitually driven by somebody else, an employee, son or daughter etc. who have become the car's keeper. The distinction really only becomes important when the car is offered for sale and you need to be sure that you have the genuine owner's consent to purchase and this is doubly important when more than one name is listed on the V5, in the case of a husband and wife who jointly own the car, for example.

Q26. What valuable information will the V5 tell me?
The familiar blue and white/blue and pink registration certificate will
help to confirm the seller's identity and address. It will also list the
former keeper's name and address (and, therefore, indirectly his phone
number) so that you can ask them about the car's mileage, condition,
period of ownership. Also listed on the right-hand side of the document
will be the date of registration of the vehicle which should tally with the
number plate suffix or prefix letter e.g. a 1985 registration will
correspond with either a "B" or a "C" prefix on the number plates. Also
recorded are engine size, vehicle identification number or VIN number;
body colour and transmission type, body plan and number of doors -
none of which should be altered without good reason. Most revealing of
all, the V5 will tell you how many former owners the car has had to
date - not encouraging if there have been many in a short time.

Q27. What details should I be looking for in the MOT certificate?
Firstly that the certificate is a valid one in terms of the amount of time
left to run before expiry and also that it relates to the vehicle
registration and VIN numbers entered at the top of the paper. General
vehicle particulars including vehicle make and age, colour, and fuel
type and mileage should where applicable, all tie in with those on the
V5 and, of course, with the vehicle itself. Lastly, ensure that the
document is signed and also embossed with the testing station's
imprint in the bottom right-hand corner.

*Q28. Why is service history so important to the vehicle's new
owner?*
A service history is not only a valuable source of information about the
car (and its running costs) for the potential buyer but, kept up to date, it
will be worth money to him when he resells in years to come. The
significance of service history has already been mentioned in **Q23**. To
reiterate briefly, it tells the new owner that a qualified, though not
necessarily main dealer, mechanic has periodically (every 6,000 miles
or six months) changed the engine oil and filter; and where applicable
regularly checked and reset the valve clearances and made
adjustments and replacements to the timing chains and belts at the
correct mileages, in addition to inspecting and tending to any other
mechanical items. Therefore, it shows that not only has the vehicle
been cared for throughout its life but also that the mileage can be
verified - this is always a strong selling point. Insist every time on a full
history when buying a used car or else never pay anywhere near the
vendor's asking price!

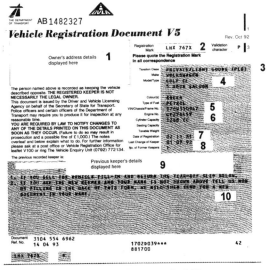

Figure 1. A sample V5.

1. **Owner (or keeper) ID**. Should agree with who the seller says he is, and also correspond with the address where the vehicle is now.
2. **Vehicle registration mark**. Should tally with both front and rear number-plates and MOT certificate, if applicable.
3. **Taxation class**. If the car was registered as a taxi or minicab prior to July 1995, this entry would say 'Hackney carriage' instead of 'private/light goods'.
4. **Make, model**. Specification (trim level) and basic body type of car: also colour and type of fuel required.
5. **Vehicle identification numbers (VINs)**. Should agree exactly with the sequence of letters and numbers embossed on the metal plate located, usually, on the front slam panel. Beware any defacing, burring or alteration of these figures either on the certificate or VIN plate itself. It often implies an 'unclean' car.
6. **Engine size**. This should correspond with both the badging on the boot or tailgate and, if applicable, old MOT certificate(s).
7. **First date of registration**. Should tally with the registration suffix or prefix letter on the number-plate (e.g., 1982 corresponds to an X or Y suffix (see also *10*).
8. **Last change of ownership**. Tells how long the current owner has had the car. If not long, ask why. Also how many former owners? Many in a short time can indicate a 'bad' car.
9. **Previous owner's address**. Contact the previous owner and ask pointed questions about the car. This can help confirm the car's true mileage and whether it has been stolen or is accident damaged.
10. Tells if the car was not new at first registration in the UK. Could be an imported model, rebuilt or even a kit car (see also *7*).

Finally, beware any 'unauthorised alterations' to the document, e.g. typewritten additions to the dates, registration number or specification. By holding the document to the light, a repeating DVLA watermark should ensure that the certificate is authentic.

Fig. 2. A sample MOT certificate (VT20).

1. **Vehicle registration number**. Check it agrees with both front and rear plates on the car.
2. **Vehicle Identification number *(VIN)***. Check agreement with the VIN plate on the car's front slam panel, inner wing or bulkhead.
3. **Certificate validity**. Look at the date of expiry on the certificate. Ask to have the car retested at your own expense if there less than ten month's MOT remaining,
4. **Mileage**. A useful clue to genuine mileage. Ensure that the mileage entered here is not greater than that recorded on the odometer - if so, the car could be clocked.
5. **General vehicle particulars**. Make sure all vehicle descriptions relate to the car.
6. **Vehicle testing station *(VTS)* details**. Is the testing station authentication stamp (station impress) both present and legible? (If not, the certificate is worthless.) Check that the VTS number corresponds with that on the authentication stamp. Also, is the MOT testing station local to the seller's home - if not, why?
7. **Signatures**. Are both the tester's name and signature present and in agreement.

Q29. Should I buy a used ex-company car over a lower mileage privately-owned example?
Generally, private one-owner cars from new represent the best value, particularly where that owner has had to pay for maintenance from his own pocket! The main problem with cars having undergone multi-ownership is that successive owners are less likely to have afforded full maintenance and this will almost certainly affect the vehicle's useful economic life.

Cars driven and maintained by the company fleets, on the other hand, and while likely to have covered huge mileages by a solitary rep., will have been serviced usually right on time with any potential problem being rectified before being allowed to develop.

Repeated motorway driving, too, is likely to have left the vehicle in much better overall condition than the considerably lower mileage privately-owned vehicle of similar type and vintage and, of course, the former should always come with a service history (see **Q31** and **Q100**).

Q30. How can I tell if a car has been driven by a private individual or whether it has been used as a taxi or minicab instead?
First make a check on the V5. Look in the top right-hand corner for the entry under taxation class. If it reads "hackney" instead of "PLG" (Private Light Goods) then the vehicle has been used as a taxi. It would also be worth speaking to the former owners in case the car had since seen private use and its taxation class changed back to PLG (although from July 1995 taxis had moved into the PLG taxation category, too). The biggest indicator of use as a taxi comes from the appearance of the interior and, in particular, high mileage. Look for:

- Very worn driver's seat and arm rests.
- Worn carpets and smooth steering wheel.
- Shiny gear lever selector (losing its gate pattern markings through repeated use).
- Tired and frayed seat belts which when tugged sharply take an eternity to return to their equilibrium positions.
- Heavily worn or scratched ignition and door locks and keys.
- Brake and clutch pedal rubbers which have started to wear down to reveal bare metal beneath.
- A dashboard showing evidence of drill holes where a radio/microphone installation would have been made.
- Doors which have started to come out of adjustment as a result of constant use.

- A prematurely threadbare carpet in the boot and scuffed loading sill marked from the many thousands of times suitcases and other heavy baggage had been repeatedly thrown in and then carelessly retrieved.
- Drill holes in either the front or rear bumpers where the local council's taxi registration plate may have been attached.
- The presence of more than one ariel
- Pale markings in the middle of the door panel areas which would suggest the recent removal of advertising stickers
- Marks in isolated spots on the roof rack guttering left where a taxi-for-hire sign had been secured.

It might also be worth mentioning that some of the more likely candidates for minicab use will be those family-sized diesel saloons and hatchbacks using a small-to-medium-sized engine and manual transmission.

Q31. Surely a high mileage car means more expensive problems?
Not necessarily and, as we saw in **Q29**, the right sort of driving could have left a car in tip top mechanical condition. Most important, then, is not the mileage reading itself, rather the *way* in which it has been earned. The proverbial little old lady covering her annual mileage of only 3,000 is likely to have done much of that in the punishing stop-start driving conditions associated with rush-hour traffic. This will have lead to particularly rapid wear on items such as the clutch and gearbox synchromesh, brake pads (through continuous use), exhaust system (because of the many cold starts), and also the engine (worn piston rings, cylinder bores, valve oil seals, and combustion chambers clogged with carbon deposits from inefficient combustion). These problems would simply not exist for the high mileage company fleet car whose regular motorway routines would have ensured that all engine fluids had been quickly brought up to temperature, thus causing minimal wear and tear, while components such as brakes, clutches and gearboxes may not have seen use for perhaps hundreds of miles at a stretch.

Public mistrust of high mileage vehicles has been slow to change and perhaps stems from the problems associated with engines from the 1960s and '70s for which 50,000 miles would have been an achievement. It has to be said, however, that engines from that era were, by and large, heavier and less fuel efficient than their 1980s and '90s counterparts and would have been - almost to an engine carburettor-fed as opposed to today's increasingly common fuel-injection units coupled to an engine management system. Today's engines also use far superior fuels, oils and lubricants than ever before. *In short, high mileage should not be an issue in one of today's cars which, if looked after, should easily surpass the 100,000 mile barrier.*

Q32. What exactly is "clocking"? Why is it a problem, and how do I know if the car I'm looking at has been clocked?
"Clocking" is the deliberate winding back or zeroing of the odometer reading to display a falsely low mileage to the potential buyer, and which is estimated to be occurring in some 30 per cent of all cars. The very act of clocking can earn the unscrupulous seller up to thousands of pounds at a stroke. Effectively, clocking appears to lengthen a car's economic life but can actually render it unsafe on the grounds that since a car is designed to adhere to a specific service schedule, as laid down by the manufacturer, certain items will require replacement at specific mileages. For example, timing belts must be replaced at around the 30-50,000 mile mark and failure to do so could result in costly engine damage.

To determine whether a car has been clocked you would need to examine the areas of the car most prone to tampering and wear. First the odometer reading: are the digits reasonably aligned - in particular the figures in both the tens of thousands and hundreds of thousands columns? Ensure, too, that the numbers have been neither painted nor taped over so that, for example, an "8" can be made to look like a "3".

Continue by examining the steering wheel position for misalignment or crookedness when the front wheels are lined up straight ahead or for missing screws that should be holding the instrument binnacle in place, both signs of hasty clocking as would be a lightly finger-marked perspex panel, the one that covers the speedometer and rev. counters and which would have needed removing when accessing the speedometer unit. Glance around the interior of the car for signs of wear (e.g. items described in **Q30**) commensurate with the odometer reading, and note any obvious external indications that the mileage might be incorrect: loud knocking noises from what would appear to be the bottom end of the engine or a continuous blue exhaust emission should not be apparent on a fairly young, low mileage example.

Q33. What other useful checks can I make to protect myself from buying a clocked car?
In addition to examining the vehicle interior for signs of wear due to excessive mileage, contact the previous owner(s) from the address

printed about halfway down on the logbook. For example if they tell you they traded the car in at 92,000 miles but the odometer now reads nearer to 52,000, then you will have your answer and can continue your search for another - genuine - vehicle. Also, if the car comes with a complete service history, take the necessary time to inspect the service book and invoices for detail and be prepared to phone the servicing garage to ask for verification of any work they've done.

Q34. Are there any particular types of car that are more likely to be clocked than others?

Generally, any prestigious or desirable high mileage-capable make or model that has a strong resale potential e.g. any BMW, Mercedes-Benz, Jaguar or Porsche is a more likely candidate for clocking than those cars lacking a strong image such as the Lada Riva, Skoda Estelle, Seat Marbella, or base model Austin Rover Metros and Maestros. Also, high mileage ex-fleet cars under five years old which, when sold at auction, could end up on the forecourts of less scrupulous dealers who might think nothing of winding back the mileage and either falsifying or discarding any accompanying service history.

Clocking is quite unlikely to have occurred in cars retailed from the forecourts of a main franchised dealer and particularly in those offered through his approved used car network.

Q35. How can clocking be stopped?

Clearly, government legislation, despite being available in abundance, has not proved particularly effective in reducing the incidence of clocking if the statistic suggested in **Q32** is anything to go by.

A longer term solution has to be one in which the car-buying public as a whole becomes educated to accept only those cars with an up-to-date service history, that is a history commencing from "day one". After all a car may have been painstakingly valeted and undergone extensive mechanical and cosmetic reconditioning prior to sale and may appear to drive and handle perfectly well. However, without the all-important history and mileage verification it should not be bought for anywhere near the top asking price. Accepting that there will always be a market for used cars without credentials, it shouldn't be too long before the majority of dealers and public will realise that the only way they can sell a car profitably will be to have bought it with a history in the first instance. Selective legislation, too, requiring the odometer reading to be accurately recorded in the relevant box on the V5 whenever the car is resold, should also do something to help close the already too-lenient loopholes that exist.

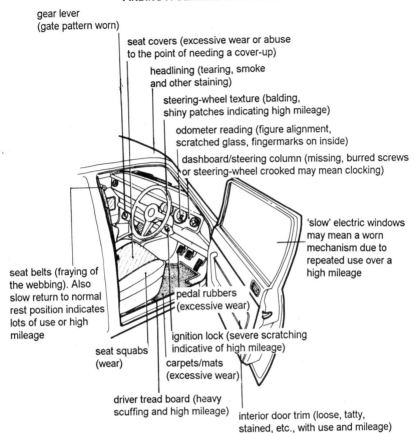

gear lever
(gate pattern worn)

seat covers (excessive wear or abuse
to the point of needing a cover-up)

headlining (tearing, smoke
and other staining)

steering-wheel texture (balding,
shiny patches indicating high mileage)

odometer reading (figure alignment,
scratched glass, fingermarks on inside)

dashboard/steering column (missing, burred screws
or steering-wheel crooked may mean clocking)

'slow' electric windows
may mean a worn
mechanism due to
repeated use over a
high mileage

seat belts (fraying of
the webbing). Also
slow return to normal
rest position indicates
lots of use or high
mileage

pedal rubbers
(excessive wear)

ignition lock (severe scratching
indicative of high mileage)

seat squabs
(wear)

carpets/mats
(excessive wear)

driver tread board (heavy
scuffing and high mileage)

interior door trim (loose, tatty,
stained, etc., with use and mileage)

Figure 3. Car interior wear to check against the odometer reading.

Q36. Won't this simply lead to an increase in service history forgeries?
Perhaps, but just as the interior of a car is unable to completely conceal evidence of clocking any more than the exterior can disguise a resprayed body panel, so there will always be signs that a history has been "doctored".

Q37. How is a service history usually doctored?
When a car is sold from new, it is issued with a service booklet (or combined service/handbook) which is stamped by the servicing dealer at the appropriate time or mileage-based interval. Some owners continue to use main dealer servicing beyond the 1-3 year warranty

period while many others opt for cheaper maintenance via a local independent garage. Either way, the service book should continue to be fully stamped as the vehicle is maintained. Any service book for a car of about five years and older ought to appear slightly dog-eared, with the inks from the rubber stamps bearing slightly different colours and shades to reflect stamping at different intervals. Clearly, a brand new-looking booklet with identical servicing stamps for a nine or ten year-old model should appear at least suspicious.

Each entry in the booklet should come with a detailed invoice to show the work carried out e.g. change of brake pads, oil and filter, timing belt adjustment etc. and without such invoices the service booklet alone cannot be relied upon. In any event, telephone the servicing dealer and have them confirm that they have indeed worked upon the vehicle. Other indications of a bogus history might include missing pages or staples in the booklet, handwritten alterations to the mileages along with the sporadic use of correction fluids.

Q38. What is meant by the term "ringing" as applied to stolen vehicles?

"Ringing" is the illegal changing of identity of a stolen car for another - usually one which has been written-off in a serious accident. Let's assume that such a car has been the subject of an insurance claim. The damaged vehicle will be sold by the insurance company for scrap at a motor salvage auction and in this way they will be able to recoup some of the money paid out in settling the claim. The wreckage would normally have fetched somewhere between about one fifth and a third of the vehicle's typical on-the-road value depending upon the exact model specification and condition. However, in cases where the amount bid is excessive for the vehicle type and condition, then this ought to be more than a little suspicious to both salvage auction staff and insurance company alike. Here, the damaged vehicle is bought at the inflated price, not with any serious intention to rebuild it, but instead for access to the all-important VIN plate, logbook and registration numbers - in other words, for the vehicle's identity.

What happens next is that an identical model (identical bodyshell, colour, engine capacity, specification and transmission type) is then stolen to order and its VIN and registration numbers replaced by those of the damaged car. A new logbook can then be applied for at a main post office, so that the stolen car appears to be the rebuilt write-off. In truth, it is a completely different car belonging to somebody else and, unsurprisingly, the vehicle is then quickly sold on to an unsuspecting buyer who may then be stopped and questioned by the police the same day, two years later or perhaps not at all. Either way, the stolen vehicle (now with the old ID) would belong to the insurance company who would have paid out on it, while the unlucky buyer might be given the option of "buying it back" again at an agreed price or else be left without redress should the original owners be identified and the vehicle reclaimed.

Q39. How can ringing be eliminated?

To stop ringing there needs to be close co-operation between the insurance companies, motor salvage auctions, DVLA and the police who, between them, would have to agree to supervise any badly accident-damaged vehicle (that they might suspect could be used in future ringing fraud) through to its complete destruction and at present, a certificate of destruction would be issued for any vehicle that is either crushed or else scrapped for parts, a copy of which is submitted to the DVLA who then freeze the vehicle's records such that its identity is taken out of circulation. A majority of crash-damaged vehicles, however, will be neither crushed nor sold only for parts and so there is currently little to prevent a (non-serious) write-off from being bought reasonably cheaply from a salvage auction, its VIN and registration numbers transferred to another, quite similar, vehicle and then sold on for a fairly sizeable profit.

Clearly what is needed is to extend the issue of the certificate of destruction to the types of vehicle particularly at risk from ringing e.g. sporty, racy, luxury and all but new models such that they, too, can be bought and used only for spare parts or else their restoration to complete roadworthiness be monitored just as carefully. Equally clear, though, is that this might involve extra effort and/or possible loss of revenue for the insurance and salvage auction companies alike.

Q40. How do I know if the vehicle I'm about to buy is stolen?

You can never be 100 per cent certain However, there is much you can do to limit the possibility.

1. *Always* purchase the car from the person named on the V5 and *always* from the address listed there in the top left-hand corner.
2. *Never* accept the seller's offer to bring the car to you or for you both to do the deal on neutral territory since if the car does turn out to be in any way suspect, you'll be left with absolutely no recourse.
3. *Ask for additional ID*, for example, a driving licence or original bill of sale for the car and, if this appears a little pushy, remember that

it is only those with something to hide that would become flustered at such a seemingly straightforward request.

4. Cross-check the VIN/chassis numbers on the aluminium plate riveted to the front slam panel of the car (although in several cases the plate may appear on the rear bulkhead while in others on an inner wing) with those entered on the logbook: there should be no defacing or alterations to either and, even if a little rusty with age, the VIN plate should appear neither brand new nor actually missing.

5. While you're looking at the logbook, ensure the general vehicular particulars such as engine capacity, colour etc. are all accurate and also that the registration plates both tally and do not look too new i.e. only very recently affixed to the car indicating that there must have been a reason to have changed them just prior to selling.

6. Telephone HPI Equifax, the police, local Citizens Advice Bureau and/or the previous owner to ensure the vehicle's status and do not buy any car for which the logbook is presently unavailable, but which will be sent on to you when it arrives back from Swansea - the chances are the vehicle (and seller) will not be genuine.

Q41. How can I tell if the vehicle I'm interested in has been particularly hard-driven?

Cars having led hard lives tend to exhibit several signs of abuse, prime candidates of which include the small sporty "hot hatch" models constructed of light bodywork and comparatively powerful engines (typically up to 1.8 litres, e.g. Escort XR3i, VW Golf GTi-16v) and frequently adorned with spoilers, bodykits, aftermarket alloy wheels and low profile tyres and body graphics screaming "soft top", "mean machine", "turbo", "16 valve" etc.; and also the genuinely sporty executive saloons, coupes and hatchbacks typically on their third or fourth owners by now.

As far as mechanical wear and tear is apparent, you would need to examine for worn suspension (leaking, ineffective shock absorbers); brake squeal and subsequent steering wheel judder (to indicate scored or warped brake discs); blue exhaust emissions (worn piston rings, valve guides, or cylinders); unevenly worn tyres; gearbox synchromesh wear (crunching upon selection), and gearbox bearing failure (again, hard use of the gears). Beware engine and gearbox oil leaks, missed services and a general lack of history, and also noisy turbochargers which clatter upon deceleration unable to deliver the necessary power on demand. A scruffy, neglected interior particularly on a fairly recent model should tell you all you need to know about the current owner's driving habits.

Q42. What are the signs that a vehicle has sustained serious accident damage?
Sometimes accident damage is easy to spot and frequently ranges from poorly-aligned body panels and coachlines, crude application of body filler, resprayed or replacement door or boot panels (together with missing engine capacity and specification badges), cracked or renewed headlights or bumper trim, or markedly uneven tyre wear to noticing that the vehicle drives wildly off-centre. Unfortunately, some of the signs of serious accident damage are simply not apparent but nonetheless insidious and might include:

- Dented or filled chassis rails and body pillars.
- Rippled, filled or repainted floorings.
- Damaged door sills.
- Dented wheel rims.
- Additional keys for ignition, doors or boot.
- Damaged overriders along with a (single) brand new registration number plate which doesn't match the origin of the other, to the potentially lethal cut-and-shut repair comprising the hasty welding of two halves of completely different cars.

If you are in any doubt about the vehicle's condition an MOT test will provide a cheap, conclusive assessment of any serious structural damage.

Q43. I've already heard of an organisation called HPI Equifax which can help save me from buying a "bad" car. Exactly what kind of information is supplied and what are its limitations?
The standard HPI check should reveal if a car has been either an insurance write-off, stolen, subject to an existing credit agreement, or which has otherwise suffered a change of identity (with the exception of a "personalised number plate" transfer) in order to conceal a suspect past e.g. a car in any or each of the above categories.

HPI was originally set up for the benefit of the garage trade to protect dealers from unwittingly buying and part-exchanging cars found to be in any one or more of the above registers and, for a nominal charge, this check will usually be one of the first the dealer will carry out. The same service is now available to the general public at £28.50 (and which includes an insurance excess) per investigation per car.

HPI has recently added further registers to its database to help with cross-checking vehicular detail and includes a **Condition Inspected** category so that were a vehicle to be written-off through accident, subsequently repaired, and then to undergo and pass an exhaustive inspection by an approved vehicle repairer, then inclusion onto this new register will reaffirm the vehicle's roadworthiness. Obviously, repaired write-off's which have not been since inspected would remain on the original Condition Alert list, indicating that further restorative work may be required. Other recent registers include confirmation of vehicular detail usually obtainable from the logbook such as colour, bodyplan and transmission and fuel types as well as first date of registration and, in respect of potentially stolen vehicles, confirmation that the VIN number (if you will provide it first) matches the car in question. HPI obtain their information from several sources:

- The Police Stolen Car Register.
- DVLA.
- Insurance companies.
- SMMT.
- Auctions and dealers.

However, it has to be said that the service can only be as good as the information is accurate. This is highlighted by the following examples:

1. *Suppose a family go on holiday for two weeks. Their car is stolen from outside their house the very next day and is quickly offered for sale to a buyer who makes a status check with HPI who, in turn, reveal that according to their records the vehicle is "clean" (or at least that no records for the car are available). Three weeks later, the buyer receives a visit from the police who are subsequently able to identify the vehicle's rightful owner. Obviously, since the car was never actually reported stolen before it was illegally sold, HPI could not be to blame for the advice they gave the buyer.*

2. *Suppose a vehicle has been seriously accident-damaged and then repaired "on the cheap" instead of being reported to the insurance company immediately after the accident. The insurance company would not therefore have been in a position to inform HPI of any collision damage to the vehicle and so the buyer clearly would be none the wiser that the vehicle could be unsafe without first insisting the car undergoes a pre-purchase MOT.*

However, the fact that one in every three cars checked by HPI has been found to be hiding at least one significant aspect of its past, suggests that £28.50 spent on a quick pre-purchase investigation would be a very sensible option. From late 1995, HPI have undertaken to indemnify the consumer in respect of any information given about a car which turns out to be misleading, provided that the vehicle is purchased within three days of receiving the HPI report.

Q44. If it's true that a car which has been used more or less exclusively around town is likely to be in poorer mechanical condition than one driven frequently on the motorways and fast A-roads, what then are the signs of heavy urban use?
The engines of vehicles driven in mainly stop-start traffic conditions tend to become "tired" and "stiff" with diminished performance and this is due, in part, to the excesses of carbon deposits which will eventually clog the cylinder combustion chambers. This can lead to erratic starting and is one of the first indications of poor engine condition. Since an engine driven this way is unable to warm up sufficiently, its oil will be working that much harder to cope with a greater amount of engine pollutants and so will become dirty much more quickly needing approximately twice the frequency of oil and filter changes. Oil leaks may be common, too, as a result of infrequent use.

Another symptom of driving under such stressful conditions is likely to be an overheating engine, indicated by an abnormally high engine temperature gauge reading. Tyres will wear faster, too, because of the increased number of directional changes at low speeds and, for a vehicle used almost exclusively around town, the chances are that the tyre sidewalls and wheel rims will have been scuffed and scraped as the driver repeatedly ran the car into the kerb when pulling over to park. Exhaust tailpipes and rear silencers - the coldest parts of the exhaust system - will rot that much quicker and tend to need earlier replacement; while gearboxes, because of the constant shifting up and down in town traffic will be far more likely to have suffered stripped synchromesh, particularly in second and third gears.

It is also generally true to say that owners who use their cars mainly in town tend not to maintain them as diligently as the longer distance motorist with service intervals spanning up to a year at a time (on account, perhaps, of the imagined better condition of the car due to the lower mileages covered). The bodywork, too, tends to suffer, dulling much quicker due to the greater effects of urban pollution and lack of frequent cleaning and for there to be a collection of parking dents, scratches and other minor paintwork aberrations amassed along the way. *In short, an exceptionally low mileage, town-only car, while at first sight appearing to be a bargain, can in fact represent a poor purchase.*

Q45. What special checks would I need to carry out on a cabriolet or convertible car?
Probably the first check is the phone call you make to your broker to check you can afford the insurance: the likelihood of theft and vandalism is very much greater than for the equivalent saloon model, particularly when the vehicle is left parked out in the street overnight.

A physical inspection should include looking for evidence of vandalism and quality of subsequent hood repairs; checking under the floor mats for damp front and rear carpets where a leaking hood might have already initiated some corrosion in the floorpan. Naturally, the hood should be both quick and convenient to operate. However, if raising and lowering is to be effected manually then you would, at the very least, need to make a check that all studs and fixings actually clip into place satisfactorily. An older convertible may by now have a near opaque rear windscreen which could also be scratched if the previous owner(s) had been careless when stowing.

Remember that convertibles will have been driven fast and hard and so you would need to bear in mind some of the checks outlined in **Q41**. During a test drive, be particularly vigilant for draughts entering the hood material due to poor sealing with the windscreen, while another potential problem, due to bad design, could be the possibility of blind spots when overtaking.

Q46. The car I'm contemplating buying has a full service history but, surely, as the vehicle is nearly ten years old, I shouldn't really need to have it serviced quite as often now - after all, if anything was going to go seriously wrong, wouldn't it have done so by now?
Not at all. Unsurprisingly, older vehicles generally do possess a greater degree of structural and mechanical deterioration than their younger counterparts and which must take into account the higher mileage and use that has been extracted from them. In fact it is more common for mechanical items such as valves, bearings, seals and bushes to have worn to the extent that either lubricants are leaking, or components are much less efficient than before and so if anything an older vehicle is going to require more maintenance and general attention. What can make an older car attractive is its lower retail price. However, this could actually work out to be a false economy in several cases

particularly since the running costs (cost of parts and repairs, service items, insurance and fuel consumption) rarely reduce with the vehicle's age.

If considering buying an older vehicle, the better bet would be to continue servicing at a local, cheaper independent garage, while looking for good used mechanical parts and body panels from breakers yards which, when needed, would do the job as well as new ones.

Q47. Should I consider buying a really cheap car - I've seen one locally, albeit a little tatty, selling for only £200 so surely I can't go wrong at that price?
You need to purchase with a lot of care. While the asking price might appear temptingly low and the car indeed a bargain, you would still need to think about the costs involved in restoring the car to full serviceability and roadworthiness. For a start there will usually be little or no service history or else road tax or MOT remaining on such low-priced 'good runners' - as they are frequently advertised - and the opportunity to inspect properly at the roadside wanting. Bear in mind that probably expensive engine or transmission, or else brake or suspension components, as well as servicing and valeting will almost certainly be necessary and, unless you'll be buying parts secondhand or at trade discounts and doing DIY-maintenance, then repairs can very quickly add up to several hundreds of pounds, thereby costing you much more than a dearer example in better condition. It is also highly unlikely that your expenditure will improve your asking price when coming to resell. *At the very least, make sure you properly test drive the car and arrange (and, if necessary, pay for) the vehicle to undergo an MOT. Although unlikely, it is possible to be lucky even at this level.*

Q48. What will a used car price guide tell me?
A used car price guide, available monthly from most newsagents, provides a good starting point for when you need to determine a ballpark price for buying or selling a vehicle, be it new or used.

For most models produced over the last ten years there will be a brief history recalling some of the more noteworthy changes and improvements made, such as engine size, trim and specification upgrades, exterior facelift etc., along with other useful information like service intervals, approximate insurance group rating, type of transmission and even overall dimensions of length and width.

The main part of the page lists the recommended trade and retail values for different ages, mileages and condition of the models listed.

Important to remember, however, is that the values quoted in the guides (of which **The Motorists'** and **Parker's** are the most popular) are by no means hard and fast and would need to be contrasted with other useful guides such as car magazines, **Exchange & Mart** and **Auto Trader** type publications along with local weekly newspapers and freesheets.

Q49. What is a "catalytic converter" and what does it do?
Essentially, a catalytic converter - or cat - is a special type of filter fitted in the end of the exhaust system nearest the driver and which acts upon the toxic emissions as they emerge from the engine. A cat is designed to treat and change the nature of the harmful hydrocarbons, carbon monoxide, and oxides of nitrogen that are produced by the combustion of fuel, so that they exit the tailpipe in a less dangerous state. The cat itself, is a sensitive filter made of ceramic material comprising a large surface area so that it can adsorb the highest volume of emissions, and uses transition metals such as Platinum (Pt) and Palladium (Pd), renowned for their powerful catalytic properties, necessary for treating them.

Some cats are more efficient than others: a three-way exhaust catalyst found in some of the more upmarket cars is, in theory, able to treat each of the above categories of emission individually and, hence, more effectively than the one- or two-way cats offered in more mainstream cars.

Q50. Which cars have them fitted?
By law, all cars manufactured and sold from January 1st, 1993 and even some cars up to a year or two before that.

Q51. What do the emissions that need treating become?
The hydrocarbons, as their name suggests, become broken down into smaller compounds of hydrogen and carbon, namely water and carbon dioxide; carbon monoxide, too, becomes oxidised to carbon dioxide, while the oxides of nitrogen become reduced to nitrogen gas. In principle, then, the car's final exhaust emissions should be even purer than the air entering the engine!

Q52. Why does unleaded petrol need to be used in "cat-equipped" cars and why must the fuel be injected rather than carburettor fed?
The idea for development of the catalytic converter as a tool for reducing harmful exhaust emissions came before the widespread

introduction of unleaded fuel and, since it was found that the lead present in petrol was effectively blocking and damaging the cat. filter, subsequent removal of much of the lead gave birth to the unleaded petrol that we have today.

It should be noted that by inadvertently filling up with even one tankful of 4-star leaded into a cat-equipped car can damage the latter and invalidate any existing warranty. For this reason, the petrol tank fuel filler neck is deliberately restricted at manufacture so as to admit only the more narrow nozzle of the unleaded petrol pump.

Since it has been long recognised that fuel injection is a more efficient means of supplying fuel to the engine than the traditional carburettor method (which feeds a fuel/air mixture to the combustion chambers), then not only is reliability, performance and exhaust emission improved, but so too is economy. Indeed, any fuel not used is simply returned to the tank via a special fuel return line. In the carburettor system, however, any surplus petrol is never recovered but simply wasted as unburned fuel which exits the tailpipe. It has been found recently that even unleaded petrol is capable of damaging the catalysts's oxygen sensor (located near the exhaust manifold) and so the fuel injection method is the only way to be absolutely certain the cat does not risk expensive contamination.

Q53. Are there any disadvantages in buying a cat-equipped model of car?

As we've already seen, the catalytic converter can be destroyed by misuse with leaded petrol, and even by using the wrong brand of petrol.

Driving over rough ground, a sleeping policeman, or through a fairly deep pool of water can be enough to shock the catalyst into premature failure, as can accidentally jolting the rear bumper against a nearby wall when parking. Cats. are also expensive to supply and fit with the job costing several hundreds of pounds for even the more everyday models.

Many mechanical warranty packages (see Chapter 5) exclude catalyst models from cover on account of their complexity and expense, and as far as environmental cleanliness is concerned, it is usual to take up to about five or so miles for the cat to achieve its optimum working temperature - those two-mile trips to the school or supermarket from cold can leave the exhaust gases as harmful as those from an equivalent non-catalysed model. Other reported drawbacks include: poor engine starts from cold, performance losses and rough engine running.

Q54. Do diesel-engined cars require a cat?

Generally not, since the diesel engine burns its fuel more efficiently than the equivalent petrol model and this, incidentally, is one of the reasons why diesels are considered cheaper to run. The main problems with diesel emissions are concerned with trying to reduce the visible soot particles and conversion of nitrogen oxides. The 1991 model VW Golf 'umwelt' diesel was one of the first engines to make use of a catalyst although - to date - few other manufacturers have been quick to follow suit.

Chapter 3

The Structural And Mechanical Assessment

Q55. Should I judge a car by its appearance?
Yes and no. If the car is a late model, high mileage example previously driven by a company rep., then it wouldn't be particularly unusual to be looking at a superficially dirty yet probably quite unworn interior, a couple of minor bodywork scratches, cracked front headlight assembly or bumper trim and perhaps evidence that a paint touch-in stick has been applied to conceal the "stone chip" rash produced by high speed driving. These are merely cosmetic imperfections which can be quite easily and cheaply remedied. If, on the other hand, the bodywork appears somewhat scruffy or else has sustained damage to the load-bearing structures, displays missing trim, a grubby, neglected interior, with torn upholstery or ceiling headlining, then these latter signs are reasonably faithful indicators as to how the car has been driven and treated generally.

Puddles of engine oil, automatic gearbox/power steering fluid or water underneath the car will confirm mechanical neglect and even the manner in which the car is now parked for display can reveal much about its former ownership. For example:

- Are any of the tyres near flat or at least well below recommended pressure?
- Is any tyre wedged awkwardly into the side of the kerb?
- Is it parked in gear?
- Is a number plate or bumper end-cap cracked or missing?

Talk to the owner himself and then ask yourself if you'd be happy to buy a car which has been owned by somebody such as him.

Q56. Which tools and accessories will I need for the inspection?
The only really "dirty hands" part of the examination involves an assessment of the engine bay and (later) vehicle underside, the remainder being taken up with judging the interior, test driving, and a brief once-over of the documentation.

You won't actually need to dismantle any part of the car, but you will be making visual and, where some mechanical components are concerned, aural interpretations as to overall soundness. Even so, you'll find use for old clothes, a good-sized dust sheet to lie on when examining underneath the car, and a small container of swarfega or washing-up liquid for washing your hands afterwards. As for tools and accessories, the following will find good practical use:

Screwdriver
Either a large flat-blade (engineer's) or cross-head (Phillips) type for the gentle probing of corroded metal, and for removing the battery cell filler caps to determine a satisfactory level of electrolyte. The flat-blade or the Phillips can also be used to remove the air filter casing securing screws where applicable so that the filter can be examined for excessive dirt.

Lint-free (non-fluffing) cloths
For wiping clean the engine and transmission oil dipsticks before meaningful readings can be taken.

Small powerful magnet
Useful, when wrapped in a handkerchief or rag, for contacting with areas of the bodywork suspected of having been filled with plastic padding. If the magnet doesn't hold then the body panel has been filled, but note that exceptions to this rule include aluminium, plastic or fibreglass (grp) panels.

Small (5" by 3") mirror
Worth taking along to help discover any holes, corrosion, filler etc. found in the floorings, door sills, door seams and other difficult-to-access areas.

Powerful torch

An absolute necessity, even in good daylight, for highlighting any structural or mechanical ills underneath the vehicle and in the recesses of the engine bay.

Tyre pressure and tread depth gauges

Essential items for any vehicle inspection kit to determine first that the tyres are adequately inflated prior to a test drive and, second, that they have sufficient tread to allow the car to be driven legally in the first place. The reading will also tell you whether the tyres are wearing evenly and also how much usable life they have left before they'll need to be replaced, which is difficult to do by visual inspection alone.

Footpump

To standardise the tyre pressures, as necessary, prior to test driving.

Pen and paper

Your inspection can take up to a couple of hours. Use a pen and paper to jot down and to be able to recall any faults which can be used as a bargaining point.

Wire brush

Useful for lightly scraping off any surface rust from the brake master cylinder assembly, door sills, door seams, wheels and any other bodywork, VIN plates and exhaust systems so that the true extent of corrosion can be assessed.

Extra £35 in cash

£27.38 for an MOT test (again, regardless of the amount of unexpired time to run), and sufficient for a couple of gallons worth of fuel for the test drive and return journey home should you decide to buy the car.

Realistic attitude

You should be looking to buy a vehicle in fairly good overall condition, a vehicle which, nonetheless, is likely to have several minor mechanical flaws which will be reflected in both its age and asking price. You should expect to have to spend *some* money, at least initially, in bringing the car up to scratch.

Q.57. What are the major mechanical components that I, as a lay person, could be reasonably expected to examine for condition?

Assuming the vehicle will be examined while standing on level ground:

- Check the engine's dipstick oil level and quality, and also starting, idling, and general running characteristics.
- Rev. the engine gently to observe the colour of the resulting exhaust emissions.
- Test the gearbox for smoothness of selection, wear in the synchromesh and, the clutch for slip and/or judder in an automatic transmission, test again for slipping, that no gears are 'missing', excessive noise during the change-ups and for correct automatic gearbox fluid level.
- Steering for slack and audible wear, and for adequate response from the power steering option if present.
- Wheel bearings for wear or lack of adjustment (a pronounced droning on turning left and right corners).
- Clicking and clonking noises due to wear in either the drive or propshafts.
- Binding or fading brakes, or for pads which have worn down so low that they've scored or warped the brake discs.

If you can manage to have the vehicle raised up on a ramp:

- The exhaust system should be examined for any insecure fixture, excessive corrosion and/or chuffing noises due to leakage of emissions and;
- The engine, gearbox, axle/differential assemblies and shock absorbers should be examined for leakage of oil and general wear.

Q.58. Which main ignition components should I examine?

Battery
Check the terminals for dry powdery deposits, frayed leads or poor earth connection (between the black or negative terminal and the bodywork) which would prevent good starting. A cracked battery casing will mean leaking electrolyte and if a white sludge has already developed at the base of the battery then this has already started to happen. Determine that the battery is not loose in its tray and that the former sits level otherwise you can expect a dead cell which will rapidly destroy the battery. Ensure that sufficient electrolyte covers each of the cell plates when you remove their tops and peer inside (however, this should be checked only when the engine is warm).

Fan belt
Check for fray and tearing at the belt's edges and for highly polished sides confirming wear and the need for replacement. An intermittent

screech upon start up tells of wear in the water pump (medium labour charges), while a continuous screech under load tells you that the belt, and hence cooling system as a whole, has been neglected.

Air filter
Unscrew the securing nuts on the filter casing and remove the paper filter element. If it's very dirty it will mean the car is long overdue for service.

HT or ignition leads (petrol models only)
From the coil to the distributor checking for excessive dirtiness, brittle or fraying wires, for poor connections(poor starting),and a cracked or porous distributor cap.

Fuel lines
Particularly from the carburettor to fuel filter for cracks and strong petrol odour.

Spark plugs (petrol models only)
Rusty or pitted spark plug bases or else ones which are smothered in oil scream infrequent maintenance.

Q59. How do I begin to examine for damage to the chassis, floorings, crossmembers, door sills and subframes ?
You will need to have the vehicle raised up on a professional hoist or inspection pit from where the underside can be viewed without obstruction and with the help of an inspection lamp or torch (such as would be the case during a routine MOT). Chassis rails will form an integral part of the floorings on the majority of post '70s cars, and should be neither twisted through accident damage nor show evidence of having been filled with plastic padding. If hasty weld marks or chalk lines are visible then the repair work has not been done properly and you would be advised to look for another car.

Floorings ought to be uniform in texture and not patched up with lumpy applications of underseal designed to conceal corrosion or damage prior to sale. Incidentally, you should also lift up the carpets in the interior to look for evidence of serious rust, rippled floorings and even freshly applied paint to try to cover a temporary repair caused, perhaps, by a rear-end shunt or by a lack of sufficient ground clearance following off-road use. Door sills also form an integral part of almost all modern vehicle structures and need to be in good condition if the MOT is to be passed.

Q60. Why is the use of body filler (or plastic padding) particularly dangerous when applied to an accident-damaged car?
The application of body filler to a car only really becomes important when applied to its structural or load-bearing areas such as those already discussed in **Q59**, that is, to chassis members, door sills and floorings, and cross members and subframe assemblies which carry some of the major mechanical components such as the engine and gearbox or axle.

Body filler applied here becomes critical for several reasons. Firstly, it means that the load-bearing members may now not be able to offer the necessary support in the event of a collision, and so not only could protection for the occupants be limited, but also the vehicle uneconomical to repair afterwards. Secondly, any union between the filler material and good bodywork is unlikely to have been the best and, upon contraction of the former during a cold winter, say, the latter will become open to further unsightly, corrosion and reduced strength. Thirdly, anybody who would be prepared to use filler to try to "repair" the structural parts of a car in this way - and knowing the effect such a hasty patch up could have on the vehicle - is, it could be surmised, equally likely to have abused his car in other ways, too: not only in missed services, lack of cleaning, kerbing and periodically overloading the tyres, but also in driving style.

Q61. How will I know if the engine is seriously worn?
You would begin by observing the engine's willingness to start. If it spins easily into life then the car has probably seen fairly frequent daily use and, depending upon driving conditions, may well be in good condition. A **blue** exhaust emission upon start up, however, tells of wear in the valve oil seals and guides, while a continuous blue emission indicates more extreme wear in the piston rings and cylinder bores - the blue colouration meaning that oil is finding its way into the combustion chambers and is being burned. Diesel engines, incidentally, may show some blue emission during warm up which can be quite normal.

Persistent knocking noises during start up or when cornering tells you of low lubrication level or, perhaps, of oil starvation altogether. Heavy knocking or rattling which appears to come from the bottom end of the engine is the more serious and is usually caused by worn big-end and/or main bearings. Remedy will be very costly in either case.

With the engine running, look under the bonnet for oil vapour escape from the oil filler cap region and, in extreme cases, from the dipstick tube. Again this may indicate piston ring wear which may be more acceptable in a high mileage example where engine compressions are expected to be lower. Engines which are lumpy upon tickover or which keep stalling, show a general need for service if noted in isolation while, if in any doubt, you could get a better idea by taking the vehicle for a compression test in which each of the cylinders' efficiencies may be determined individually. You would need to suspect an engine in reasonably poor condition to insist upon such a test although the problem could also be identified as one in which a single cylinder's power is well down or perhaps a cylinder head gasket has started to blow.

If a diesel engine is worn, symptoms will include continuous black exhaust emission (worn injectors and/or distributor pump), oil leaks as well as a generally noisy, sluggish ride.

Q62. Can the condition of the exhaust tailpipe tell me much about the state of the engine?
Absolutely. A badly rusted tailpipe (with the rest of the system in a reasonably uncorroded state) will mean the engine has engaged in frequent cold starts in what will probably have been rush hour style traffic i.e. continuous stopping and starting. This will soon cause excessive engine wear and so, even if the car's overall mileage is low, it will have been hard-earned with several expensive repairs to the whole drive train imminent.

Look at the colour inside the tailpipe: black powdery deposits mean that the fuel mixture is too rich and, while little more than a simple service adjustment, this can cause long term engine damage if left unchecked. Gummy black deposits, however, confirm that the engine has been burning oil (look again for blue exhaust emissions); whilst a crusty white scale tells of too lean an ignition mixture and that engine overheating may have already begun. If the cylinder head gasket has blown (see **Q68**), then a continuous cloudy white emission or even a trickle of water will be apparent long after the engine has had time to warm up. If the tailpipe appears to periodically "belch" then it is likely there is either a misfire e.g. one spark plug fouled or on a higher-mileage car, that the valves are worn and will need attention.

Q63. Are there any simple, straightforward checks I can make on the car's steering and suspension?
Rotate the steering wheel slowly to full right lock observing the motion of the front offside roadwheel as you do so. In a standard rack and pinion steering system there should be little more than about 3/4" of visible play in the steering wheel that is, before the roadwheel begins

to turn in sympathy. Some cars use a steering gearbox assembly, cars such as the larger Vauxhalls, BMW's and older Japanese models, which employs a slightly more complex system of steering joints. This means that in conducting the test described above, up to about 2" of slack is usually permissible. Do listen out for audible clunking or groaning noises which manifest themselves as the wheel is rotated from side to side. In systems using power assisted steering (PAS), such groaning usually points to wear in the steering pump (and you would need also to check the steering fluid in the pump reservoir for low level and, by now, possibly brown grey colouration). In non-assisted systems (i.e. those cars without power steering), the same "groaning" could point to worn steering column bushes or universal joints meaning the system could need expensive stripping down to repair.

Lastly, if you can gain access to underneath the vehicle's front end, look and feel for torn steering rack gaitors which house the steering ball joints. If a rubber gaitor is damaged then you might expect a bill for a new rack.

As far as the vehicle's suspension is concerned, do the following test: depress each of the car's wing corners in turn. In each case the wing should generally bounce up a little, depress again very slightly and then come to rest. For the shock absorbers to be worn to any great extent, you would have to witness continued bouncing; note, too, that exaggerated wear and which would cause much 'wallowing' during the test drive. If you can arrange, again, to have the vehicle stationed over an inspection pit, then you will be able to examine directly for oil leaking along the struts themselves as proof of wear in the dampers and that the pair would need replacement.

Q64. What, specifically, should I be looking for when buying a diesel car?

Almost all the structural and mechanical checks that applied to petrol-engined models will apply equally to diesels. In addition, though, you're looking for excesses of black exhaust smoke which is really wasted fuel and illustrates the need for (expensive) overhaul of the fuel injection system. A diesel will produce some clattering noises upon start up which should settle down when the vehicle is under load i.e. being driven. If starting is difficult or if irregular noises outside of the usual diesel warm-up are apparent, then this should be treated with suspicion.

As with petrol models, a full service history is not only desirable but invaluable in helping support claims of careful ownership and the service records should indicate roughly *twice* the frequency of oil and filter - as well as fuel filter - changes as the corresponding petrol model. Do check the V5 again, for evidence that the car might have been registered for use as a taxi: high mileage and a tough mechanical life will have been the inevitable result.

Q65. *Is it safe to buy a remould or part-worn tyre?*
Whilst all remoulded tyres - secondhand tyres given renewed tread and sidewalls - would have to pass a minimum British Standard (BSI AU144b), it is as well to remember that not only may product quality vary considerably, but they are not recommended for continued high-speed motoring. A frequent problem experienced with remould tyres is that of 'tread separation' caused by poor remanufacture with the new tread starting to peel away from the old carcass. At the very least, this can result in rapid and uneven surface treadwear and/or consistent vibration experienced at all driving speeds. Other problems with remoulds stem from their limited life expectancy relative to a new tyre, the more frequent requirement for wheel balancing, and also that combining both remould and original tyres on the same axle can even result in potential MOT failure. A huge majority of reputable tyre dealers refuse to sell them at all.

'Part-worn' tyres, on the other hand, are simply used tyres for which you will have little knowledge of their age or driving history. And as cheap as they may appear, can a potentially dangerous tyre really be worth buying at any price? When funds are low, I would recommend purchasing a new - if budget-priced - tyre every time.

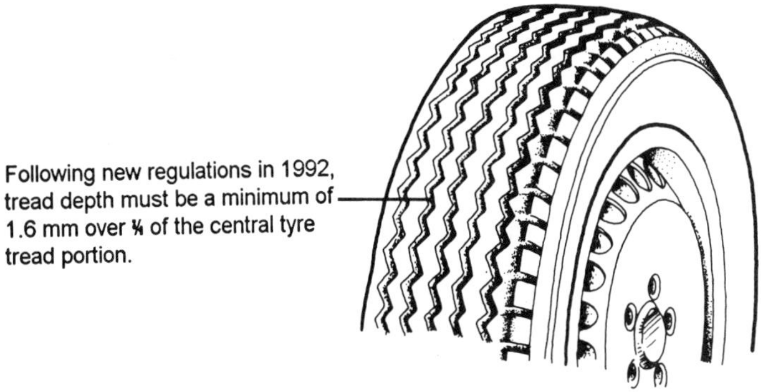

Following new regulations in 1992, tread depth must be a minimum of 1.6 mm over ¾ of the central tyre tread portion.

Figure 4. The tyre tread area and tread wear indicator (TWI).

Q66. I'm confused about the law as it applies to tyre tread depth.
Since January 1st 1992, all tyres must, by law, have a minimum tread depth of 1.6 mm across ¾ of the central tyre tread surface along with at least visible tread over the remaining shoulder bands, and this applies to the spare, too, if one is present. Ensure that each of the tyres on your prospective model have at least 3 mm tread.

Many tyres use a built-in tread wear indicator (or TWI) buried into the tread pattern itself so that when the TWI becomes visible, it means that the tread depth is down to exactly the 1.6 mm legal limit and the tyre must be replaced. Should a tyre be worn to below this minimum depth, it can attract for the owner a fine of currently up to £250 per single tyre.

Q67. I've heard about "wheel balancing" and "front-end alignment". What do they mean exactly and why are they so important?
Because of the imperfections inherent in a tyre at manufacture and also because of general wear, the tyre/wheel assembly requires regular balancing at strategic points on its rim which is carried out by affixing small weights. A tyre which is out of balance tends to grip the road less effectively, sets up unpleasant vibrations in the car at speed, and also produces a disproportionate increase in tyre wear and fuel consumption.

Out-of-balance wheels usually manifest themselves by a shaking of the steering wheel as the car accelerates through the 45-55 mph range and again at about 90 mph.

Wheel alignment or tracking on the other hand, has more to do with the correct angling of the front (and in some cars the rear) wheels and takes account of the necessary slack built into the suspension so that the vehicle is able to corner and handle as intended. Badly misaligned wheels, which can be caused by 'kerbing' the car at speed, through accident damage, worn suspension or simply from prolonged driving on unevenly inflated tyres will tend to show by producing a characteristic scrubbing or feathering around the outer front tyre shoulders. Other symptoms include excessive fuel consumption and a tendency for the car to veer off-centre as it progresses along an otherwise straight flat road affected little by camber. A good tyre dealer will be able to balance all four wheels and realign the front pair for about £35 all-in, while the tyres themselves should be checked for correct track and balance at least every six months.

Q68. What is the specific function of the cylinder head gasket; what are the symptoms of failure, and why is it such a potentially expensive item to replace?

The cylinder head gasket is a very tough thin layer of rubber/metal composite joining the cylinder head to the block and keeps the oil and water separate in each. If the gasket is defective or if the engine overheats through insufficient coolant level or from continued driving on an already too-slack alternator drive belt, it can split allowing the oil in the cylinder head to flow through to and become mixed with the coolant in the water jacket passages of the engine block and vice versa. This in turn means that cooling will be inefficient, leading to eventual overheating while the engine compressions will be diminished, reducing both power and performance, and causing bad cold starts and increased fuel consumption. If the situation is allowed to continue unchecked, overheating can lead to warpage of the cylinder head which may then need expensive re-machining or outright replacement depending upon the extent of the damage already done.

You would need to observe from many signs that the head gasket is blowing before jumping to conclusions since similar symptoms can be produced by condensation in the oil as a result of the car being driven only very short distances in winter when the engine has had insufficient time to properly warm up.

Begin by examining the engine oil on the dipstick. If there are very many water droplets mixed in with the oil or indeed, if the oil has taken on the appearance of a grey-green sludge which doesn't disappear after something like a thirty or so mile uninterrupted motorway run, then this is a first indication that oil and water have started to mix. Remove the oil filler cap and look for the same gooey mush on the cap underside and in the oil filler neck. Likewise, if the coolant in the radiator or expansion tank is decidedly low or of "oily" texture, then this is another clue, as would be coolant losses in which the route of escape is by no means obvious. During a test drive you will need to keep an eye on the engine temperature gauge - if the reading climbs too high too quickly (or does not rise at all when already well into a journey), then the possibilities of overheating and probable head gasket failure are high.

Replacing the head gasket involves removal of the cylinder head, scraping off the old gasket, examining for damage or head distortion and putting in its place a new one for which much of the expense will be labour. On an older, rear wheel drive and longitudinally-oriented four cylinder-in-line engine, access to the cylinder head is quite straightforward and usually trouble-free. However, the difficulties arise with the more complex "vee" engine configurations - the V6, V8 and V12 designs comprising more than one cylinder head and, therefore, two gaskets to be renewed - in addition to the plumbing of local auxilliaries such as air conditioning and power steering systems which must be dismantled and then reassembled adding to the overall costs of the job.

Chapter 4

The Test Drive

Q69. Do I really need to test drive the car and, if so, how long should I spend?
A test drive is an absolutely essential part of the vehicle inspection for three very good reasons:

1. In preparing his car to near showroom condition, the owner might have been successful in disguising some serious mechanical shortfall which, if it became apparent, would render the car unattractive at his asking price and you may not be able to tell this without first driving the car. Besides, finding some real or imagined faults and then using them as a bargaining point is very much a part of what the test drive should be about.
2. No two examples of the same car are ever exactly alike (even if they were identical in engine size, mileage, and date of registration), since their driving histories will have been unique to the individuals that owned them and it is almost certain that wear will have occurred to quite different extents in different components - such is the nature of used cars.
3. When the seller insists on playing chauffeur, who is going to be driving the vehicle on a daily basis - you or he? Insist on at least a half hour's drive which, on the one hand, will be necessary to bring the engine lubricants up to full working temperature, and also to encompass a fair mix of roads from motorways and fast A-roads, to heavy town traffic, busy junctions and, where possible, country lanes/ B-roads. This is necessary so that by the end of the drive you

will have gained a fair impression of how the vehicle behaves over a whole variety of road-going conditions.

Q70. What preliminary checks should I make before I test drive the car?

Remember that since the new car is quite likely to be a different make or at least different model from your current one, the main drawback will be a lack of familiarity whether in size, shape or overall dimensions, gear selection gate pattern, steering response or brake pressure required, clutch biting point, ride quality and suspension characteristics or general driving position and dashboard instrumentation layout. These are sufficiently good reasons for you to take your time when, at least initially, you may not be aware of any expensive problems brewing.

Before you do take to the road, however, make a final check on the tyre pressures. If they vary by more than even a few pounds from the recommended (or from each other), then you will not be able to make an accurate appraisal of the car's steering, braking and handling characteristics. Make sure you're aware of any overhanging boot or bonnet length or protruding wheel arches and, finally, do be absolutely certain that you are adequately insured to drive the car. A dealer will usually provide insurance as a matter of course, although most policies will offer a minimum of third party cover. Check this is acceptable to the seller first, though.

Q71. What am I actually testing for while out on the road?

You'll no doubt be appraising the new car's plus points, but you will also need to pay particular attention to what's wrong with it, even if only something quite minor such as lower than full engine compression, above average wear in the cabin interior or any non-essential dashboard instrumentation that no longer functions. There will always be imperfections in any used car and money needed to be spent in putting them right, and one objective of the drive will be to exaggerate these slightly.

Listen again to how the engine sounds upon start up. Does it rapidly spin into life, an indication of frequent daily use or is the engine slow to turn over? How quickly does the engine note settle down to tickover? A lumpy, uneven idle can point to lack of maintenance, premature wear or abuse. Did you notice any prolonged untoward rattling noises (oil starvation) and, if so, were these from the top end (not quite so bad), or more likely from deep within the cylinder block (expensive)?

While on the road and having built up some speed, you will want to attempt an emergency stop when convenient and again at lower speeds to be satisfied that the vehicle brakes in a straight line without undue squeal or screech. Again you will have determined whether you needed to apply only light brake pedal pressure, whether the pedal appeared soft and spongy (leaks) or else needed to use its full travel reserves to bring the car to a halt.

Next the gears. With manual transmission note the ease of selection and whether gear changes were accompanied by crunching (worn synchromesh due to hard frequent use, or low oil level in cars such as the Mini whose engine and gearbox share a common sump); or whether the gear lever remained in the chosen gear or else jumped back into neutral indicating a worn mechanism. With automatics, you'll be anticipating reasonably smooth change-ups, with only minimal delay in selecting from, say, neutral (N) to drive (D). Be sure to try reverse gear and be warned if the delay in selecting, and also the reverse manouevre itself, takes more than about two or three seconds. It could mean a gearbox oil leak and expensive remedy (see also **Q74**).

What about general handling and behaviour over potholes and when taking corners - are road shocks effectively absorbed or did you experience exaggerated wallowing and crashing over bumps? Acceleration should be smooth and even from rest without any hesitancy or flat spots (although not a major problem), and were both engine roar and general road noise acceptable? It was stated earlier that a fairly long test drive would be necessary in order to maintain the engine lubricants at normal working temperatures as quickly as possible so that any mechanical ills highlighted by leaks or noise will manifest themselves in good time for you to make a decision.

You will need to study the dashboard instrumentation from time to time to be sure that any readings and warnings are meaningful. In general, be satisfied that the engine temperature gauge is responding, while not actually moving into the red and if an oil pressure gauge is fitted, that there is at least some reading at idle and certainly not a reduction of pressure at speed when the engine is fully warmed. If only an oil pressure warning light is fitted, then remember it should extinguish immediately the engine fires and never return or even flicker on and off while the engine is running. If it does, then pull over and switch the engine off without delay and have the cause investigated.

Q72. How do I test for a slipping clutch?

There are two tests you can do, both of which are reasonably straightforward and conclusive:

1. With the handbrake on and the engine idling, select a high gear such as third or fourth and then release the handbrake, let the clutch slowly out and try to move away from rest. If the clutch is in healthy condition, the vehicle should stall without delay.
2. While out on the road and driving up an incline, note when you change down to a lower gear, whether the engine revs rise markedly (increased engine noise) yet the actual road speed remains much the same (i.e. progress up the slope was very slow). Provided you had been in a sufficiently low gear ratio this would be indicative of a slipping clutch.

Q73. What extra checks must I carry out on a four-wheel drive (or off-road) vehicle?

In addition to the basic checks outlined already, you will need to have examined the underside of the vehicle for damage and corrosion resulting specifically from off-road use. For example, twisted or buckled door sills, dented floorings, damaged chassis members etc. Inspect the tyres, too, for evidence of uneven wear which, in an extreme case, can point to (expensive) misalignment of the four-wheel drive system. Study the underside carefully for leaking axles and drive shafts, both of which would produce some noise during the test drive, and try to determine whether the vehicle used not only a towbar at the rear, but also a winch at the front - in this case the subsequent tolls on the drivetrain could make replacement parts very costly.

Lastly, whether you intend to use the vehicle off-road or not, do be sure you are able to access both high and low ratio (four wheel drive) gears by use of the transfer gearbox lever next to the main gearshift. Lack of service may have caused partial seizure of the mechanism.

Q74. Some people say that automatic gearboxes should be avoided because of their high expense. Is this true and, how do I test one for condition?

It is true that when new there may be a price differential of several hundred pounds between an otherwise identical pair of models, one equipped with a manual gearbox and the other an automatic. However, when properly looked after there is no reason why the automatic gearbox should not be able to last the lifetime of the car.

Automatics do require some attention, principally that the transmission fluid level is maintained at the correct dipstick level, that its colour is the proper shade of red and that a high mileage - say, 90,000 miles - example has, where appropriate, had its transmission filter replaced. Unlike its manual counterpart, it is not common for the clutches in an automatic gearbox to wear out and require periodic replacement.

To check the transmission fluid level in an automatic, ensure first of all that the engine is properly warm i.e. after a drive of fifteen miles or so and, with the engine still running and the car stationed upon level ground, select park (P), remove the automatic gearbox dipstick, wipe clean and reinsert, then read again in the normal way. A healthy transmission unit will show a deep red, slightly viscous, liquid at somewhere between the high and low dipstick markings. Conversely, transmission fluid which is actually pink will tell you of water contamination (expensive). An orange-brown appearance means burnt transmission and an equally expensive overhaul required telling you to leave the car well alone and begin looking for another.

Q75. Is it worth a second look under the bonnet after the test drive?
It is, if for no other reason than to re-appraise any of the engine bay components or lubricant levels you had initially suspected of being below par and for which a second check would now be worthwhile.

Better still, make sure you remember to park the car over a reasonably dry hardstanding area while you wait for subsequently leaks to emerge. You can expect a few droplets of oil from an older engine, automatic gearbox or axle and particularly after a long, fast motorway run. Of course, there are some tests that you can only conduct when the engine has been allowed to fully warm up - for example, examining the cooling system for seepage from the radiator, hoses or water pump; and the automatic gearbox fluid level reading as described in **Q74.**

Q76. What do the recent MOT regulations mean for windscreen and rearview mirrors?
Windscreens should be clean and free from cracks or chips that might impair the driver's view of the road ahead. For the purpose of the MOT test, the windscreen is divided into two broad zones as shown in Figure 5. If a crack appeared inside of the shaded area of zone A, it would have to be containable within a 10 mm diameter and, if within the unshaded area of zone B (passenger side), a windscreen defect should

not exceed a 40 mm diameter. If not then the car would probably fail the test. Door and rear view mirrors must be both fully adjustable and free of cracks or blemishes that would again impair driver vision.

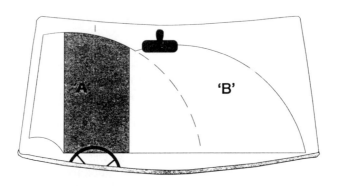

Figure 5. Windscreen MOT regulations.

Q77. What should I do when I'm happy with the test drive and think I want to buy the car?
Even though the vehicle might have stood up fairly well to tough structural and mechanical prodding and a fairly rigorous road test, I would always advise that you seek a second opinion. Arrange with the seller beforehand to let you take the car to an MOT testing station of your choice (and for which a main dealer for the make would be most preferable) and, for under £30, you will have had a truly independent assessment of any hidden accident damage not easily discernible from your own visual checks with the vehicle grounded. *This will also confirm that the car is actually roadworthy at the time of your purchase*. Having the car re-MOT'd can be a useful bargaining ploy in respect of any items that fail, despite that there may yet be several months current MOT left to expire. Also, unless the vehicle has no MOT at all, you can further increase your bargaining position by offering to pay for the test yourself.

Q78. Which professional inspection services are available to examine a car for me, and what will they cost?
There are several avenues open to you ranging from the AA and RAC motoring organisations, a franchised dealer or local independent

garage to an independent vehicle inspection service. With the AA and RAC, you will be charged according to engine size and type of car and can pay anywhere up to about £300. For this you will receive a detailed report summarising the bodywork condition, mechanical and road checks on a par with those already described above, together with a free HPI Equifax vehicle status check. If you're spending even a few thousand pounds on a car, then this type of service can prove a very cheap insurance indeed. On the downside, it could take a few days to book an appointment so you would need to know if the car will still be available for sale in the meantime.

Bear in mind, too, that dealer stock on some forecourts may have already been inspected by one of the above organisations, for which an accompanying report will be available, and so this will have saved you the initial inspection outlay.

Q79. What about alternative vehicle inspection services I can use?
As already hinted, the franchised main dealers, independent local garages, and private vehicle inspectors should be willing to offer an unbiased examination every bit as conclusive as the AA or RAC although prices will probably depend upon the level of detail you require. *Always insist upon the vehicle's underside being properly examined for damage or poor repair.*

The MOT, as a valuable bargaining tool has already been discussed in some detail in **Q77** and, again, is the only one which is able to legally confirm the vehicle's roadworthiness. Its limitations are such that neither the cooling system, gearbox, nor engine condition (except in respect of exhaust emission levels) - and each potentially very expensive items to repair - would be appraised and that the test itself is really only valid for the period of its own duration.

Chapter 5

Used Cars And The Law

Q80. Is there a minimum code of conduct I can expect from a dealer when I'm buying a used car?
In order to satisfy the Code of Practice laid down by the Office of Fair Trading in conjunction with the Society of Motor Manufacturers and Traders (SMMT), the Retail Motor Industry Federation (RMIF), and Scottish Motor Trade Association (SMTA) a dealer, whether franchised or one of the smaller independents must, for any car that he sells, provide:

- (Or at least allow) adequate inspection facilities.
- Any vehicle over three years old with a current MOT test certificate and ensure that any other relevant documentation such as service history, repair bills, invoices or handbook etc. are handed on with the car.
- Adequate documentary proof of the vehicle's mileage (if the mileage is to be advertised).
- A pre-delivery inspection report for the car and a copy for the customer's retention.
- No misleading statements about the car (see **Q81**).

Q81. So what basic rights do I have when I purchase a second-hand car?
You have recourse via the law whether buying from a dealer or a private individual although the extent of protection will depend upon from whom you make your purchase. If you buy from a dealer, you are protected by the Sale of Goods Act (recently amended by the Sale and Supply of Goods Act 1994) which means he will have to guarantee that:

- The car is fit for its purpose.
- It is of satisfactory quality.
- Any statements or claims he makes about the car are accurate and true.

As an example of the first condition, let's assume you specified, quite clearly, that you needed a car capable of covering at least a thousand miles a week; accommodating up to six passengers at a time and which would also have room to carry bulky land survey equipment such as theodolites and levels, tripods and outdoor clothing, and tow a trailer on a fairly regular basis. Obviously, the dealer will be failing in his duty if he then went on to sell you a 1980 1.0 litre two-door Austin Metro which had covered nearly 110,000 miles on its original engine.

In the second instance, "satisfactory quality" means that for the price you will be paying for the car, this should be reflected in its condition once such factors as the age, mileage, number of former owners and any readily apparent bodywork or mechanical defects have been allowed for. All this is designed to protect you from buying what, on first impression, appears to be a used vehicle in good serviceable condition but which in reality is little more than a structural or mechanical time bomb waiting to explode. It has to be said, however, that this is a somewhat difficult condition to enforce because of the vehicle's description as being 'used' and, as such, there will always be some worn or defective items that will require replacement sooner or later. It will be largely up to you to decide what is or is not good overall value when you conduct your examination of the vehicle.

In the third instance, let's say you had proof (for example, from an advertisement) that the car you were looking at was a 'Ghia x' specification model. If it was later revealed to be an 'L' model only then you may have grounds for a claim. Likewise, you would also have a case to argue, if you were told that the vehicle had recently had a new gearbox (for which you might reasonably expect to have been supplied and installed by a main dealer or else transmission specialist) only to find, in fact, that the "new" gearbox turned out to have been a secondhand unit sourced from a scrap yard. The issue is not that the gearbox might be serviceable and trouble-free but that you were specifically told the component was new and had believed this to be reflected in the car's overall asking price.

Your redress when buying privately, however, will be limited to the seller's description of the car (and also reassurance in respect of certain elements of its roadworthiness). For instance, if the seller was prepared to warrant the odometer reading which could be later proved otherwise, and if he then offered little co-operation, you would be able to start a claim through the small claims court. However, had the seller stated in his advertisement: "recorded mileage", or simply not mentioned the mileage at all, then his description of the car - in respect of its mileage - will not have been inaccurate, and any subsequent claim would very likely produce little result. For protection when buying a car at auction please see **Chapter 7 - Motor Vehicle Auctions**).

Q82. How do I make a claim against a dealer if the car I've bought has a serious fault?

First of all you will need to determine whether the claim you wish to make is a valid one (see **Q83**). If it is, for example, an intermittent transmission or significant steering fault (which didn't manifest itself during the test drive, and is one which you couldn't easily have deduced as a lay person) then simply return the car to the dealer with proof of the problem, and try to enforce your legal rights! It could be that concealed wear has rendered the vehicle unroadworthy - despite it having been awarded a brand new MOT - and, provided there were sufficient grounds, you may be able to make a successful claim there, too. Whatever, the dealer may well concede liability for the fault and offer you either part or total mechanical or financial redress.

Should the dealer be at fault, yet prove unco-operative with your request for help without good reason then you will need to have the faulty component inspected by an independent specialist, which need not necessarily be expensive. Have them confirm in writing both the nature and extent of the fault, and at the same time giving an idea of how long the problem appears to have existed and also what it would cost to rectify. Obtain two such reports if you can. Return to the dealer and if he is still unhelpful, you must put in writing this time the steps you have already taken and that you will need the fault to be put right within a matter of about ten days, allowing adequate time for the dealer to make the necessary arrangements with you.

Should the dealer still not have even contacted you by this time then you should go ahead and have the repairs carried out and pay for them, keeping a receipt for the work as evidence. Then it will be a matter of pursuing a claim against the dealer through the small claims court in which you would have to issue a summons on him. If your claim is successful and, provided the dealer has the means to pay, you should receive a settlement for the repair of the faulty component. It has to be said, however, that it would be quite rare for a dealer not to want to at least discuss the legal position or else offer some redress at one of the opportunities you had provided.

Q83. Are there any instances in which I would not be able to claim for faults?

You would not be able to seek redress from a dealer if the faults discovered included any that you should have been able to diagnose as a lay person e.g. a balding tyre, dented or visibly corroded body panels, cracked windscreen or torn upholstery. Neither would you be able to claim if the dealer had already disclosed a fault to you prior to your buying the car, nor if you'd had the vehicle inspected professionally and the engineer had overlooked something during his examination.

Q84. Are there any other special conditions that I must observe in order to improve my chances of a successful claim?

You should return the vehicle to the dealer the moment you notice any fault which you think to be significant. This protects you in two ways:

1. It shows that you are not happy to accept the car whilst it is in this (defective) condition and,
2. That it is highly unlikely that the problem could have originated whilst in your possession.

Naturally, were you to complain and return the car some six months after purchase, this would be too late to claim even under the terms of the Sale of Goods Act. Returning with the same problem inside of two weeks, however, would vastly improve your chances of a settlement. Written notice of dates and times at which the fault(s) occurred along with copies of any correspondence with the dealer will be helpful, if and when the matter needs to go further.

Q85. Do I have any legal protection if I buy a car on finance or via a credit agreement generally?

If you purchase a car on finance, HP or certain other credit arrangements, you may be protected against any breach of the Misrepresentation or Supply of Goods (Implied Terms) Act or from a dealer suddenly going out of business, since the finance house in question will have assumed joint liability for the transaction. This is one of the few benefits of buying a car on credit as opposed to paying by cash or via an overdraft or (personal) loan from a bank or building society.

Q86. How do I pursue a claim against a private seller?

When buying a car privately, your protection under the Sale of Goods Act is limited to the seller's verbal and/or written description of the vehicle. It would be a good idea, then, to retain any advertisement that drew your attention to the vehicle in the first place should any wording need to be contested later.

A car may be described as being faster, more economical or durable or perhaps more popular than it actually is, however, provided this falls within the remit of mere sales chat then the seller would not be breaking the law. For instance, being told that a particular car, *"Costs next to nothing to run"*, or that, *"It'll never break down"* is clearly intended to be only figurative. Stating, on the other hand, that replacing the cracked exhaust manifold will be no more than a half hour job or that the exhaust system is new when in fact it was installed over ten months ago are clearly misleading statements. It would be important, nonetheless, to weigh up the relative costs of any defective items or the impact of any unsubstantiated claims before rushing to contact the local Trading Standards Authority. A seller may have been foolish enough to guarantee complete reliability in the model he is selling you, only for you to find that the battery had run flat by the very next day. In this situation, it might be more appropriate to appeal to the seller's sense of fair play in trying to recover some of the £30-50 a new battery would cost, rather than suffer the inconvenience and aggravation of frayed tempers, red tape, wasted time or financial losses that would be incurred in the event of the battery needing an engineer's inspection and the matter then not even making it to court. Describing an engine as being a 2.8 litre reconditioned unit, however, when the supplying firm of engine remanufacturers can later show you a copy of an original invoice to prove they actually installed a 2.3 litre engine, would provide you with all the necessary back up to confront the seller's exaggerated claims prior to pursuing a claim for compensation.

A private individual must also guarantee the vehicle's roadworthiness in respect of the Road Traffic Act which covers steering, brakes, lights, tyres and reflectors. However, roadworthiness would also have to extend to some of the more obvious items such as overall structural soundness and efficiency of the shock absorbers, to the proper functioning of the horn. *Insisting on taking the car for a pre-purchase MOT at your own expense ought to minimise the odds of having to return it shortly afterwards for what could turn out to be an avoidable time-consuming complaint.*

Q87. Is it worth buying a warranty?
This depends largely on the type of warranty cover you purchase, how much you pay for it, what it excludes and, equally important, from whom you buy it.

There is a significant difference between the genuine one-to-three year warranty offered by a manufacturer and which covers all structural and mechanical defects (except tyre abuses) as a result of poor workmanship or materials - but which excludes defects due to accident damage or neglect on the part of the owner - and the less comprehensive package offered by an insurance company.

Among the conditions of the manufacturer's warranty that bind you will be for you to ensure that the vehicle is serviced in accordance with the dealer's schedule i.e. that you have it serviced at a main dealership at the required intervals and that genuine manufacturer service parts are used e.g. Motorcraft parts for Ford cars, Unipart for Rovers etc.

With an insurance company-underwritten warranty, also known as a mechanical breakdown insurance or MBI package, however, cover will almost always be limited to an upper claim limit and maximum number of items while exclusions will typically encompass:

- Turbochargers.
- Exhausts and catalytic converters.
- All wear and tear.
- Exotic high performance models (e.g. Jensens and BMW M-series cars),

and many other mechanical items including:

- Water pumps.
- Timing chains.
- Starter motors that were already on the vehicle prior to the commencement of cover!

In other instances, there exists a betterment clause taking into account that if a component such as an eight year old gearbox needs replacing under warranty, then that item will have accumulated eight years worth of wear and so the policyholder will be expected to contribute something towards the cost of the brand new unit in respect of the wear present before the failure occurred. Many older cars will be either exempt from cover altogether or else attract a higher premium or suffer reduced cover to the point that the warranty may not actually be worth having. *Considering, too, that much of the warranty premium can be dealer commission, I would nearly always advise, in such cases, that the cost of the warranty be negotiated out of the asking price and that the same money be spent instead on a full service after purchase with a further interim and major service to follow that.*

Other restrictions might include that the vehicle never be used for minicabbing; that you be tied to servicing by a dealer of the warranty company's choice and/or, if you read the small print carefully, that at each service the invoice and stamped service history booklet be forwarded on to the warranty company as proof that the required conditions are being met.

If you really do require warranty cover, try to choose a package endorsed by a motor trade association such as the SMMT or AA and whose policy terms and conditions are likely to be that much fairer and easier to comprehend than could be said for several other so-called warranties on the market. Finally, it should be noted that any printed guarantee or warranty package is *additional* to your basic statutory rights under the Sale of Goods Act and it may be prudent in some cases to claim under the latter first where the dealer may be open to negotiation in respect of both parts and labour costs.

Q88. Can you list any trade or other professional bodies which might be able to help me in the event of my needing to make a claim?
A few of the more immediately useful organisations able to advise on making dealer and related motoring claims include:

AA
Fanum House
Basingstoke, Hants
RG21 2EA
0161 4856000 Legal Advice (members only)
0345 500 610 Vehicle Inspections

Association of British Insurers
51 Gresham Street
London
EC2V 7HQ
0171 600 3333

British Insurance Brokers Association
14 Bevis Marks
London
EC3A 7NT
0171 623 9043

Citizens' Advice Bureau
Look in phone directory for nearest branch

Crown Prosecution Service (Public Enquiries)
0171 273 8152

Finance and Leasing Association
Code of Practice Section
18 Upper Grosvenor Street
London
W1X 9PB
0171 491 2783 Credit and finance problems

HPI Equifax (HPI register checks)
01722 422422

Legal Aid
29/37 Red Lion Square
London
WC1R 4PP
0171 405 6991

Motor Insurers Bureau (MIB)
152 Silbury Boulevard
Central Milton Keynes
MK9 1NB
01908 240000 Uninsured and untraced drivers

Office of Fair Trading
For local Trading Standards Office
0171 242 2858

RAC
0345 300400 (legal services for members)
0345 336600 (technical services)

Retail Motor Industry Federation (RMI)
9 North Street
Rugby
CV21 2AB
01788 576465 Garage and car problems

Scottish Motor Trade Association (SMMT)
0131 225 3643

Small Claims Court
Look in phone directory for nearest court

Society of Motor Auctions
P. O. Box 13
Wilmslow PDO
Cheshire
SK9 1LL
01625 536937 For complaints concerning motor auctions

Society of Motor Manufacturers & Traders
Forbes House
Halk Street
London
SW1X 7QS
0171 235 7000 New car and warranty problems

Vehicle Builders and Repairers Association
Belmont House
Finkle Lane
Gildersome
Leeds
LS27 7TW
0113 2538333 Accident repairs

Vehicle Inspectorate
Church Hill Industrial Estate
Lancing
West Sussex
BN15 8TU
01903 753305 MOT problems

For a more in depth look at motoring law, you are advised to read, **WHEELS OF JUSTICE: the motorist's guide to the law**, by Duncan Callow, legal expert with **What Car?** magazine. Also published by Otter Publications, the details are at the back of this book.

"Mr Bowles, we think you've tampered with the odometer because you tried to sell a 1972 Ford Cortina with only 12 miles on the clock, and you say in your defence that it only had one owner to date, a careful lady driver with........agoraphobia!"

Chapter 6

Coping With Dealers
And Sellers

Q89. Are all car dealers very much the same or can I secure a better deal from a particular type of dealer?

Not all dealers are the same and, as we had summarised in **Q3**, they fall into two main categories:

1. The franchised main agents offering top of the range stock in their approved used car schemes e.g. Citroen Hallmark, and Ford Direct, and which provide many tangible customer benefits.
2. The smaller independent, several of which may engage in corner-cutting and deceit if their main concerns do not include good reputation, customer satisfaction, or repeat business.

This is only a rule of thumb however and there are some very good smaller outfits able to offer high quality cars and a back up service second to none and, by contrast, there exist main dealers whose overall quality of service would leave something to be desired.

If you are thinking about buying from one of the independents, look for one that boasts affiliation to a recognised trade body such as the SMMT, RMI or SMTA, who, whilst acting principally in the interests of the dealer, will be able to offer recourse to the buyer in the event of a dispute which cannot be resolved amicably. It would be true to say, in general, that member garages of the RMI, SMMT etc. are under slightly greater pressure to offer higher standards of service than some of the independents that continue to trade according to their own arbitrary standards.

Figure 6. SMMT, SMTA, RMI, AA and RAC motor trade association symbols (please note that none of these organisations are in any way connected with this publication).

Q90. I don't enjoy all the haggling and negotiating - shouldn't I just tell the dealer straightaway the car I'm after so that he'll be able to help me much more quickly?
From the moment you walk onto a dealer forecourt you are undergoing "qualification" by the salesman, which means that he'll be evaluating you as a prospect in terms of your appearance, speech and background, existing car (as a potential trade-in) and, most important, whether or not you'll be likely to buy a car from him today, and so it is not surprising to learn that, after dealing with many thousands of potential customers like yourself over the years, the salesman will have developed a kind of sixth sense as to your seriousness of intention to buy (and which might help explain, incidentally, why when you've been interested in only browsing at the cars on a forecourt, the salesman has made little effort to come out and try to sell to you).

It would be much better to confide in the salesman only your general requirements without going into details of specific cars or prices that you had in mind and this applies particularly when you believe you've spotted the very car you think you'd like. In this case do not express too much interest in the vehicle. Instead make it the very last one you go to take a look at because if the salesman suspects a high level of interest now then why would he need to be generous at all when serious negotiations begin?

There is little doubt that there'll be several other vehicles on the forecourt that the salesman might prefer to sell you and so this is another good reason to have a firm idea of (and also to have researched) the sort of car you'll buy before you even set foot near the dealership. After all, if you've got the money in your pocket (sic) and a desire to purchase a car as soon as possible, then you will already have put yourself at a distinct disadvantage if you have not prepared adequately. *Any* car can be made to look economical, good value, a sensible purchase etc. when you're at your most vulnerable.

In short, do your homework first, know the specific model(s) that interest you, seek them out and play down your interest in them. Don't tell the salesman any more than he needs to know.

Q91. Should I pay too much attention to the windscreen sticker descriptions. I mean, a dealer isn't going to say anything bad about the cars is he?
By all means use the sticker descriptions as a guide, but remember that it's often what *isn't* said that can be most revealing. After all, what exactly is meant by "low" or "average" mileage: average for a company car driver of 60,000 a year or average for a private motorist? And of the "only two previous owners" claim - were either of them particularly diligent when it came to properly maintaining the vehicle on time? "Stereo" can mean any make but a good one, while the promise of an "MOT" can be a short one with perhaps only six or so weeks left to run. Finally, what would you make of the claim that the vehicle has been, "well- maintained"? Does it imply a full service history for the car from new, or merely that the car has been tarted up prior to sale? Look for meaningful statements only, such as: new MOT, f.s.h (full service history), one owner from new, and ensure that all claims can be adequately backed-up by genuine documentation.

Q92. The dealer tells me the car has been serviced by him recently - how do I know this to be true?
Evidence of recent servicing (or not) will never be far away. Start by opening the bonnet and withdrawing the engine oil dipstick (ask where this is if you're not sure). Recently-changed oil will look and remain a light golden brown colour for the first few hundred miles and ought to be level with the dipstick's "maximum" mark. Likewise, the oil filter should've been replaced at the same time and will clearly not have been done if it appears heavily smeared with dried-on streaks of oil. Only when the engine has been switched off and is completely stationary, examine the fan belt (alternator drive belt) for condition.

Inspect for frays or cracks at the belt's edges and, to determine that its tension is approximately correct, depress the longest stretch of belt at its centre with your thumb. If the belt deflects more than about half an inch it is too slack, and if less, then it is too tight and the job has not been done properly. Any other drive belts e.g. for power steering or air conditioning should also be free of defects. They are usually not expensive items to replace.

Radiator hoses ought to be examined for perishing or bulge once the engine is warm although, even when cold, a recently-renewed top hose and clips should be readily apparent. With the engine cold, remove the radiator or expansion tank cap and be sure that the coolant inside reflects a strong antifreeze colour and not the dirty rust-coloured appearance of a long-neglected cooling system. Spark plugs are another cheap routine replacement item - good for some 12,000 miles, usually - and new ones will show a shiny plug end where they enter the engine cylinder head. Of course, definition of the term "service" can vary from one dealer to the next. To some, at least all of the above will have been carried out while, to others, a service may mean little more than an oil change followed by a quick rub down of the bodywork with a bucket and sponge. Have the dealer state **in writing** the items checked and replaced.

Q93. The person I'm buying from says he cannot produce an actual stamped service history booklet for the car, but insists he's done all the maintenance himself. Again, how do I know he's telling the truth?
The simple way to determine whether or not the car has been frequently and periodically maintained is by the depth of answer you receive to some fairly superficial questions. You're not trying to catch the seller out, nor attempting to cram the techniques of car maintenance overnight, but it shouldn't be too difficult to discern the difference between maintenance which has been genuinely carried out and mere waffle. Ask the seller which brands of oil he used and also the viscosity ratings. Ask, too, about the make of air and oil filters he used and what they each cost. Any hesitancy in the answers will tell you whether you need ask any further questions. Servicing involves a lot more than merely changing a few lubricants and filters, and so you will need to determine how, and how often, for example, the valve clearances had been adjusted, what attention the carburettor or fuel injection system had received, and what were the typical spark plug gap settings.

Also, at what intervals were the axle and transmission oils checked and topped up and then drained and refilled? You will also want to know about any similar routines for the cooling, suspension and braking systems and whether any receipts for replacement parts are available. *If a seller is prepared to guarantee full DIY maintenance as a means of attaining his asking price then surely you have every right to probe into his methods as far as you wish.*

Q94. How can I negotiate a better final price?

Despite what you might read and hear in some of the motoring press concerning the way that certain "insiders", posing as ordinary car-buying customers, seem able to use all manner of ploys to beat a hardened salesman into submission, in reality there will come a point at which the dealer will not or cannot afford to discount his retail price much further whether you are able to meet it or not.

Frequently, the way to swing the sale in your favour is to obtain from the dealer some relatively low-cost extras (low cost to him) but which would be of immense immediate benefit to you. For example, by asking the dealer to, *"throw in a new MOT"* for the car, this will cost him little, while giving you some, at least theoretical, peace of mind. Six months road tax, too, would transform what is perhaps an already attractively-priced £5,000 used car into one which is ready to drive away today.

Besides, it could be argued that taxing a car prior to sale is a dealer's responsibility anyway. Consider a full service which might ordinarily cost you in the region of £100-150 but, to the dealer, only a small fraction of this cost. Finally, if it is a warranty you preferred, have the salesman include a 12-month MBI package or else upgrade the standard of cover already provided. *Look, then, for concealed benefits that won't be reflected in the final asking price.*

Q95. How can I improve my part-exchange deal?

Firstly, by being realistic. Bear in mind that you will normally only achieve a "trade" price unless your car is something of a rarity or else popular that is, in high demand yet relatively low circulation. Seek the opinions of several dealers and be prepared to act quickly when you're quoted a good price and, if you can, try to establish a part-exchange price on your car without specifying which model you would be trading in against. This will give you an idea of the vehicle's basic trade value and one which you can then check in the used car price guides.

Obviously, presentation counts for a great deal where part-exchanging is concerned. If your car has been professionally valeted beforehand it means the less preparations the dealer will have to make before he resells it. If you opt to clean the car yourself, do ensure that you pay particular attention to:

- The door shuts and inner body pillars.
- Driver and passenger treadboards.
- The bonnet and boot underside areas and boot carpet.
- The inside of the glasswork.
- The between-instrument crevices in the dashboard.

Also, the following will vastly improve your chances of the highest part-exchange you could hope for:

- Carefully remove any unsightly rust from the bodywork with an abrasive strip.
- Touch-in any unsightly stone chips accumulated through high mileage.
- Repolish any existing brightwork (window surrounds, chrome, etc.).
- Put the vehicle through an early MOT.

Personally, I would advise that if you can manage to have your car prepared to this standard and if it is able to survive a few hard test drives, that you forget the idea of part-exchanging and try for a cash discount instead. You should gain further still if you hold out for a private sale which will almost always fetch you a better price.

Q96. Any other tips?
For a start, there is nothing a dealer likes less than a time-waster and so if you can show that you're actually serious about wanting to buy a car and have the means to arrange the necessary finance **today**, then you will be more than halfway to having the dealer on your side. Some dealers work on a monthly or quarterly commission cycle, so that were you to begin your negotiations for the car on the very last day of that period (e.g. June or September 30th) then, the salesman may be prepared to be even more generous with his discounting if he was very keen to receive his bonus for reaching his sales targets.

Also, do put in the necessary time and effort to compare the different deals offered at the various forecourts in your area. You may be quite pleased, in the end, that you didn't settle for the first car you looked at.

Chapter 7

Motor Vehicle Auctions

Q97. Are all motor auctions basically the same?

While it is true that they are each in the business of auctioning motor vehicles, it is equally true that their standards and also range of cars offered may vary markedly. The major trade centres such as the ADT, National Car Auctions and Central Motor Auctions networks deal in huge volumes of generally newer stock, many entries coming from the company fleets, and vehicle hire/rental companies - and even some overspill from manufacturers' "dealer-only" auctions - which dispose of their stock periodically.

In the smaller independent auction, there are usually fewer cars for sale, and are typically a little older. Most will not have been entered direct from company fleets or other volume user of motor vehicles, an important point as we have already seen in **Q3**.

If in doubt as to how to choose a reputable auction site, look for affiliation to the Society of Motor Auctions (SMA), members of which are obliged to observe at least a minimum code of conduct.

Q98. What are the general categories of motor auction sale?

For stock of up to about five years old and entered with mechanical warranty are described "sold all good" and will, as the term implies, carry a guarantee on the major mechanical components namely, the engine, transmission (including the clutch and axle), steering and brakes.

The mileage on a vehicle in this category will be warranted if it comes with a complete service history, and it is on such cars that an after-sale test drive is permitted and the risk of buying a bad example the lowest.

The other category is the "sold as seen" entry which is over five years old and purchased with any and all plus points or latent faults together as a complete package. Due to the age of the vehicles, no mechanical warranty or test drive will be offered and, if a major component were to expire shortly afterwards, then that is all a part of the risk you would have to take in buying a vehicle at a trade price.

Q99. How can I save money by buying a car at auction?

Well, far from being the dumping grounds for worn out, over-the-hill motors that no dealer worthy of his name would risk peddling from a forecourt, buying the right sort of car at the right auction (e.g. an ex-fleet model such as a Sierra, Mondeo, Cavalier, or Vectra, etc., entered directly at a major trade centre) can represent a vast saving to the private individual if not a bargain, since it is possible that the very same lot, if bought from a dealer only a week later, could cost about another 30 or so per cent - the extra premium reflecting in many cases little more than the car having been valeted and a warranty added prior to sale.

And as we saw in **Q3**, the other saving for the private buyer derives from the vast range of vehicles assembled under one roof, thus minimising the phoning around and chasing up of cars from advertisements and dealer forecourts, the bulk of which would either have already been sold or which might prove unsuitable for any number of reasons. There is something to be said, too, for the level of consumer protection afforded the auction buyer such that there is recourse in buying a stolen vehicle or insurance write-off, or one on which finance was still outstanding or which had undergone a change of identity in order to conceal a shady past.

On the contrary, auction sites - both good and bad - are the traditional stamping grounds of used car dealers, the very places from which they purchase their stock to retail on to the public.

Q100. What are the main drawbacks of buying a car at auction?

The fact that you would be unable to vet the current owner or seller in order to determine some of the more important aspects of the vehicle's history, puts you at a disadvantage over the equivalent private purchase, but not an awful lot more so than if you were to buy the car from a dealer because at least (at auction) you would have seen it in its 'unprepared' state. Thoroughly inspecting the vehicle can be a problem, however, since often little more than a brief once-over of the visible areas such as bodywork, tyres, exhaust tailpipe and windscreen lot ticket (or engineer's test report) is ever really possible while the vehicles are tightly shoe-horned into the auction compound.

The other main gamble is in buying the car without mechanical warranty (and therefore, in the "sold as seen" category) so that while the vehicle might well look to be in good general condition, it could in fact be hiding serious mechanical deficiencies. In other words, that "bargain" price of £1,500 you paid for a car having the equivalent retail of £2,200, might turn out to be needing at least a further £1,800 in repairs to make it fully serviceable.

Q101. You said that inspection of a vehicle whilst in the auction compound is likely to be very limited, but is there nothing else I can do to determine whether it's a good or bad car before I purchase?

Well, in addition to examining the lot ticket affixed under the windscreen, you must listen very carefully to the auctioneer's description of the car while it queues its turn for the ring. He'll tell you, for example:

- Who had owned the vehicle formerly (e.g. a business, private owner, etc.).
- Whether it had been in *direct* by the previous keeper(s).
- Of any known mechanical faults disclosed prior to entry.
- Whether it had served as a former police car or other utility vehicle.
- Or if the vehicle had been an insurance write-off or even a finance company repossession.

Whilst the car is idling and just before the auctioneer begins his description of it, you might request the driver pops the bonnet to allow you to inspect the engine bay and, in particular, the quality and colour of lubricant on the dipstick (you won't have the time to take an accurate reading, simply to note that the oil isn't actually black or totally absent). If the car has automatic transmission, have the driver select reverse gear while you listen and await any malfunctions (see **Q74**) and, if the steering is power-assisted, note any particularly loud groaning noises over and above the inevitable hiss when full lock is applied. Try also, to listen as carefully as you can to the engine and exhaust idle notes. In this way you will be able to make an additional, rapid assessment of a car which, had you not, might later have cost you very dearly.

Q102. Apart from the entries from the company fleets and car hire firms, where do all the cars actually come from?
Many come from dealers who are overstocked with trade-ins and pre-registration or nearly new-models recording little more than a delivery mileage, and who need to turn them into cash. Others may represent finance company repossessions on cars which are again but a few months old. Others still can come from banks, building societies and even from official receivers and bailiffs disposing of vehicles on behalf of organisations like the Inland Revenue or Customs and Excise. In fact cars selling at auction can be there for any number of reasons, entered by anybody who needs to turn their car into cash quickly, cleanly (without comeback) and with as little effort as possible. This also helps explain why the cars are frequently very cheap to buy.

Q103. I've seen a car I want at auction. Can you describe the bidding procedure?
First of all, set yourself a realistic upper price limit for the car (typically 25 per cent below its current dealer forecourt price) over and above which you will not be tempted to bid. You're buying at auction in order to make a considerable saving on a car that you hope will give plenty of service, and yet not pay too near top retail for what, so far, would have to be described as a vehicle in quite unknown condition.
    The auctioneer will usually only accept up to two bids at any one time and so it is important that he clearly sees you make your initial gambit after which subsequent bidding can be coded and therefore more low key. Being a private buyer you should be able to put in a higher bid than the trade, secure the car and still have made a sizeable saving. Try to enter the running only when everybody else has started to drop out (i.e. when the bid intervals are becoming longer and increments as low as £10 or so) and, if possible, as the hammer is going down for the last time. Go to the rostrum and pay your 10 per cent deposit or £500, whichever is the greater, then make the necessary arrangements to pay the balance and collect the car at the first convenience.

Q104. Will there be any extras that I'll have to pay over and above the final bid price?
Yes. Most reputable auction houses will insist on your taking out an indemnity of up to about £40 for the standard HPI check detailed in **Q43** and which in some cases may cover you against the car having been clocked i.e. if a warranted mileage was later found to have been misrepresented. Furthermore, the term of the indemnity could be

without limit. There may also be extra storage costs incurred should you fail to pay for or collect your purchase within the agreed time limits.

Q105. So what determines the final price a typical lot is likely to sell for?

The final bid price fetched by any lot can be subject to many factors - even two identical models selling from the same auction hall and on the same day, may not necessarily achieve the same price. Clearly, final values will depend upon:

- The range of stock present.
- Their lot number allocations and therefore the order in which they file into the ring.
- Their engine sizes, colours and general desirability.
- The popularity and geographical location of the site.
- Even the weather can influence the size of the attendance!

To be certain of securing a car for the lowest possible bid, however, I would always recommend you visit a major auction site and on a weekday morning when the majority of attendees will be trade with a genuine interest in keeping the bidding low. By contrast, weekend and evening auction sales tend to attract more of the public which, in turn, generally escalates the values of the individual lots.

Q106. What is meant by a 'provisional' or private treaty sale?

A provisional sale is one in which the reserve price for any particular lot has almost (but not quite) been met by the last bid on the vehicle. The auction staff will then try to negotiate a final price on behalf of the seller and last bidder. In the event that an acceptable final price cannot be agreed and the vehicle remains unsold, the seller would still have to pay the full entry fee charged.

Q107. Am I able to purchase a warranty or guarantee for a car at auction?

In addition to the standard £25-40 HPI/Auction Indemnity fee and/or mechanical warranty that automatically comes with a car in the "sold all good" category, it is possible, at some auctions, to purchase a further warranty endorsed by a motor organisation such as the AA provided the vehicle is no older than about seven years and has a warranted mileage of under 100,000. Warranty cover can start from about £40.

Q108. Can I purchase a van or light commercial vehicle at auction?
Yes, however, it should be remembered that most light commercials offered for sale will be either diesels or turbo-diesels rather than petrol models, and that it is customary to pay a VAT surcharge on top of any successful bid. Try to choose an auction group such as ADT which, again, offers specific van and light commercial vehicle sales days. Entries will come in the form of finance company repossessions (not the best category of vehicle from which to buy), manufacturer's contract hire lines, ex-rental, Post Office and Royal Mail fleets, ex-British Rail and BT Escort/Maestro/Transit stock, and other vehicles disposed of periodically by the local borough and county councils. It would be helpful to obtain a recent copy of **Which Van?** or similar publication to help keep a check on trade prices before you buy.

Q109. How do I go about selling my own car at auction?
Simply telephone the auction site first and find out their conditions of entry and times for when it would be convenient to bring the vehicle in. As a private seller you'll pay about £30 to enter your car, along with an auctioneer's commission of about 10 per cent upon successful sale. At some auctions an extra fee will be payable should you wish - or be permitted - to set a reserve (or minimum price below which you would not be prepared to sell the vehicle). You will need to bring along all the documentation:

- V5.
- Current and past MOT's if applicable.
- Service history, if applicable.
- Any other invoices for repairs and maintenance etc. which could help improve the final sum you'll receive.

At the same time you will be requested to fill in a simple entry form detailing some of the car's registration and ownership particulars including whether the mileage can be verified, whether the car has seen use as a taxi, whether ever accident-damaged or if finance is still outstanding etc.
   Do take the necessary time to clean the car inside and out since a tidy, and apparently well-looked after example will create a better impression and, it is hoped, a better price. Finally, it can even help to be present at the time of sale in the event of the car not reaching its reserve and so being knocked down provisionally.

Chapter 8

Looking After Your Car

Q110. What should I do once I've bought my "new" car?
The first thing would be to phone your insurance company before you even return to the car to drive home. If your uninsured car was to be involved in a collision - regardless of who was actually to blame - you would have no rights to make a claim and the damage for which you might have to pay to somebody (or for the damage to their property), could well run into several thousands of pounds, let alone the cost of repairs to your own vehicle.

Next, if there is little evidence to suggest a recent full service (or any service history details for the vehicle at all) then it would be best to see to it now. It is not uncommon for a buyer to have acquired a particular car and then, over the ensuing months, find that his racy new model for which he'd had so many expectations has repeatedly had to go back to a garage for several service items and major and minor adjustments e.g. a change of spark plugs one week, a new air filter the next; loose starter motor the very day after that, followed by the need for a new battery, distributor and ignition timing reset during the following weeks. Not surprisingly, the owner quickly begins to see his new car (and often the make in general, now) as unreliable and costly when a full service carried out shortly after the sale would have been cheaper and might have told an altogether different story for the next 6,000 miles!

If a full service cannot be done right now, then of major importance will be an oil and filter change (although don't cut corners in oil quality), a new set of spark plugs (or at the very least an inspection of the present set followed by any cleaning or re-gapping as necessary) and, for cars using an OHC engine - most modern front wheel drives - a new timing or cambelt which would then need to be religiously changed every 35,000 miles or so.

The other advantage of a service done now is that you will be getting the benefit of the servicing mechanic's experience. After all, in the course of your inspection you might have overlooked a fraying fuel line, low power steering fluid level or, perhaps a worn alternator fan belt buried under the tangle of air conditioning trunking/compressor unit, and can have the matter rectified now before it develops into a major overheating problem.

Of course, you will also have insisted beforehand that the garage stamp the service booklet that came with the car as well as providing you with an invoice breakdown detailing the work carried out at that mileage.

Q111. What else?
Once you are satisfied that the recent MOT/garage overhaul has identified and corrected most of the faults and that you've decided you definitely want to keep the car, you should immediately register it in your name using the V5 and send it off to the DVLA at Swansea. The fine for failing to do so is currently running at up to £1,000.

Q112. What can I do to protect my car from a break-in or theft?
By ensuring, first of all, that whenever you leave your car unattended you have locked the doors and boot, closed the windows and sunroof and removed all valuables from display (e.g. even loose change from the dashboard). This at least ought to limit any undue attention from the opportunist thief.

There are several highly visual anti-theft devices you can buy, many of which owe their effectiveness to their complexity and the amount of time it would take a thief to overcome them.

* Stoploks and krookloks that you fit between the steering wheel and clutch or brake pedals start at under £20, with wheelclamps beginning at about £60.
* Driver and passenger-door deadlocks which help prevent access to the interior even when, say, a side-window has been smashed in order to make off with the stereo can represent good value.
* A BSI-approved alarm (or immobiliser) if sufficiently loud and/or sophisticated to prevent the thief from actually driving the car away.

- Security window etching, in which each of the windows is marked with the vehicle's registration or engine numbers has the advantage of making the thief think twice about stealing the car and then having to replace all the glasswork before he could sell it on again - or else having to rely on selling to a quite unobservant buyer!
- And while there are as yet no official statistics available for the numbers of vehicles actually saved from theft, it is probably a good idea to register your car with the local police "vehicle watch" scheme which is free to join and one which might make a difference.

However, since no single device can reasonably do any more than deter the more casual theft (i.e. if someone really wants your car, they will probably be successful), then it is perhaps as well to combine as many of the above methods for greatest peace of mind.

MORE FROM OTTER PUBLICATIONS.......

WHEELS OF JUSTICE (1 899053 02 6, £5.95, 128 pp) by *Duncan Callow*, is aimed at all, including the legal profession, who would like to find out more about how they would stand legally in any given motoring situation. The easy to understand style makes it extremely accessible and contains a useful glossary of terms to clearly spell out all the legal jargon used. *WHEELS OF JUSTICE* is intended as a practical handbook and draws upon many of the author's experiences, both professional and personal. Key areas covered include:

- Insurance
- The MOT and vehicle safety
- Accidents and dealing with their aftermath
- Drink driving and related offences
- The major motoring offences
- The court process
- The fixed penalty system and the penalty points system
- Parking offences and wheel clamping
- Basic motorcycle law
- Driving on the continent
- Buying a used car

"This highly readable law book covers all aspects of driving...useful facts abound". AutoExpress.

"The driver's bible". The News of the World.

BEHIND THE WHEEL: the learner driver's handbook (1 899053 04 2, 264 pp, £7.95), also by *Graham Yuill*, is a step-by-step, highly illustrated handbook. Now into its fourth edition, the book **features a full colour section and questions and answers to help the learner driver learn to drive and pass the theory driving test.** *BEHIND THE WHEEL* will teach the reader all aspects of driving and road safety in 20 easy lessons The teaching methods used are those laid down by The Driving Standards Agency. A completely up-to-date section on trams has also been included. Finally the events of the driving test day are outlined in full with useful advice and tips. **Endorsed by the Driving Instructors Association.**

"Anyone who is learning to drive, or teaching someone else, will appreciate Behind the Wheel". Woman and Home.

PILLARS OF JUSTICE, the homeowner's guide to the law (1 899053 03 4, 192 pp, £6.95) guides the layman through the many legal aspects of purchasing, owning and running a home. Given that a home will be the most expensive purchase of our lives, a working knowledge of the law as it affects us is critical. The easy to understand language makes the book very accessible and a helpful glossary of terms explains the legal jargon. The key areas covered include:

- The legal aspects of property ownership
- Buying and selling a house and the associated pitfalls
- Insurance
- Building, improving and extending your property
- Dealing with the utility companies
- Renting out your home
- Dealing with the neighbours
- Dealing with tradesmen/consumer law generally
- Home security
- The legal aspects of debt

WORKING FOR JUSTICE: the employee's guide to the law (1 899053 06 9, 224 pp, £7.95), aimed at all employees, is a guide through the many legal aspects of working for somebody else. Now that employment can no longer be taken for granted, a well-informed knowledge of the law as it affects us is critical. The easy to understand language makes the book extremely accessible and a helpful glossary of terms explains the legal jargon used. *WORKING FOR JUSTICE* is intended as a practical handbook. The key areas covered include:

- Employment status
- Pay
- Unfair dismissal
- Wrongful dismissal
- Redundancy
- Disciplinary matters
- Discrimination
- Trade Union membership
- Maternity
- Health and safety
- Transfer of undertakings
- Employment law in Northern Ireland

ADVERTISING FOR THE SMALL BUSINESS: how to reach maximum sales for minimum cost (1 899053 08 5, 160 pp, £7.95). Sales are the lifeblood of any business. If you are self-employed, running a small business or handling the marketing for a small company, then this book is for you. *ADVERTISING FOR THE SMALL BUSINESS* is a practical guide and provides an introduction to advertising for small businesses where budgets may be limited but sales vital in an increasingly competitive environment. The book explains about:

- The purpose of advertising
- Classified advertisements
- Display advertising
- Other forms of advertising
- Sales letters
- Direct response
- Sales promotions and point-of-sale advertising
- Public relations

HITTING THE HEADLINES! : how to get great publicity (1 899053 05 X, 160 pp, £7.95) takes the stress out of dealing with the press. This invaluable, step-by-step book offers a wealth of easily understood, commonsense advice on the best way to get your news into print, how to deal confidently with reporter enquiries and how to maximise the impact of good publicity. Insider tips include:

- The most effective way to approach news editors
- How to place advertising to reach the maximum audience
- How to ensure your press release becomes a headline story
- How to lessen the damage of bad or unwanted publicity

Whether you are a hard-pressed charity fund-raiser, a sports club seeking to raise its profile or a small company wanting to launch its own sales/PR campaign, *HITTING THE HEADLINES!* answers all the questions you've ever had about getting great publicity from newspapers, radio stations and TV news services.

Iain Pattison has been a journalist for twenty years. He is a media consultant of industry and holds two national journalism awards.

We are living in an age when violence against car-drivers and theft from cars is on the increase. **ARRIVE ALIVE** (1 899053 00 X, £4.95, 96pp) is aimed at all who are concerned about their own personal safety on the road and behind the wheel. This step-by-step, easily understood book will teach the reader how to keep safe, how to recognise and escape attacks, how to prevent car theft and how to deal with all other problem situations before they become deadly emergencies. The book is completely up-to-date, including information on car bombs and The Channel Tunnel. It explains all the latest protective devices and teaches the best defensive driving techniques. In addition, detailed aerial-view diagrams illustrate the situations and manoeuvres described.

"Packed with information on every aspect of safety for motorists, it's essential reading". Woman' Own.

DRIVING FOR INSTRUCTORS: a practical training guide (1 899053 09 3, £7.95 128 pp) *Graham Yuill,* is a handbook for both experienced and new driving instructors to help them pass the upgraded ADI check test. The teaching methods used are those laid down by The Driving Standards Agency. **Endorsed by the Driving Instructors Association.**

"This guide is a must for potential and fully qualified Approved Driving Instructors. There is a wealth of information here for those who wish to improve their instructional skills". John E. Ayland, Chief Examiner DIAmond Advanced Motorists.

How to order:-
Through your local bookshop or in case of difficulty, please send a cheque made payable to Otter Publications, 5. Mosse Gardens, Fishbourne, Chichester, West Sussex, PO19 3PQ, ☎ 01243 539106.

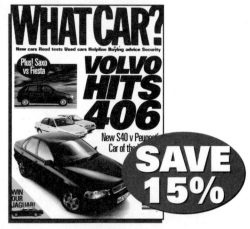